Making a difference

Standing UP in a Sit-Down World

is easier than you think

Merrilee Boyack

DESERET
BOOK

SALT LAKE CITY, UTAH

DESERET BOOK is a registered trademark of Deseret Book Company.

Visit us at DeseretBook.com

Library of Congress Cataloging-in-Publication Data

Boyack, Merrilee Browne, author.
    Standing up in a sit-down world / Merrilee Boyack.
        pages cm.
    Includes bibliographical references and index.
    ISBN 978-1-60907-057-1 (paperbound)
1. Conduct of life. 2. Voluntarism—Religious aspects—The Church of Jesus Christ of Latter-day Saints. 3. Courage—Religious aspects—The Church of Jesus Christ of Latter-day Saints. I. Title.
    BX8656.B69 2012
    248.4'89332—dc23   2012003219

Printed in the United States of America
Malloy Lithographing Incorporated, Ann Arbor, MI

10 9 8 7 6 5 4 3 2 1

To my mother and father,
who taught me to stand up and to serve

Contents

Acknowledgments

I'd like to thank Lisa Mangum, who is an outstanding editor, and Jana Erickson, who has been unfailingly supportive. Many thanks to Deseret Book for once again extending to me the opportunity to teach and share.

CHAPTER 1

Decide to Be a Giver

"Inasmuch as ye have done it unto one of the least of these my brethren, ye have done it unto me."

—Matthew 25:40

I have a strange hobby. Now it might have something to do with my career—I am an estate-planning attorney, and I work with families to help them be prepared for death or disability—but I think it has more to do with my fascination with what people choose to do with their lives.

My morbid hobby is reading the obituaries. My mother used to read them, and somehow I began to do the same. I don't read the whole article, usually, but I do read the headlines. They make for fascinating reading. Who was this person? What did they choose to do with their life?

One day I was reading the obituary headlines to my husband, Steve, who does *not* share my strange fascination, and I burst out laughing. There in big bold print was an obituary headline I'd never seen before. After listing the person's name and age, it said, "Expert bowler." Expert bowler! I was amazed. Can you imagine living for seventy-six years and the most important thing someone could say about you was that you were an "expert bowler"? I couldn't believe it.

I asked my husband what his obituary would say. He mumbled an "I don't really care," but I thought about it for a minute. I think Steve's headline should read, "Steve Boyack, 104, beloved Scout leader, dies on top of Mt. Whitney." Steve was a Scoutmaster for eleven years and a Scout leader for more than thirty years, and I am grateful for his service not only to our four sons but to all those boys and men to whom he has given his time and energy, so that seems like an appropriate headline.

I want you to take a minute and think about this question: *What will your obituary say?* Will it say "Mary, expert shopper" or "Mary, PTA volunteer"? Will it say "Jim, devoted employee" or "Jim, devoted grandfather"? It's rather sobering to think about reducing your life to a handful of words, but it is also extremely enlightening.

To quote Montaigne, "The glorious masterpiece of man is to live to purpose; all other things . . . are but little appendices and props."[1]

So what is your purpose? What are you doing here on this planet? And, most important, have you chosen to be a taker or a giver?

Takers and Givers

Takers and givers are very different kinds of people. Takers are never truly happy. They can never take enough to fill that hole in their soul. They are glued to their workplace at the expense of everything else: take, take, take. They roam the malls: take, take, take. They are busy people who don't have time for anyone or anything else.

Takers expect to be rich. They expect to have lives of total happiness. They expect to be perfect, in a worldly way. They expect to have power and influence. They expect to have it all. They may be rich, but the money will never be fulfilling to them because it will never be enough. They will never be happy enough or perfect enough, and someone will always have more power or influence than they have. Takers live miserable, small little lives, never extending their view beyond their own selfish desires. Some takers sit back and expect everything to be given to them, with no thought to contributing. Takers will never find happiness in that which does not fill their soul, and the only thing their obituaries will say is "expert taker."

Now givers are quite another story. I want to tell you about Millie. (That's not her real name, but this is a true story.) I knew Millie quite well. She lived in a little house in the poorer section of our city. She had many children. She never drove a car. She didn't have much money, and both her appearance and her dress were plain. Most people would have said there was absolutely nothing outstanding about Millie. Except for one thing—Millie was a giver.

Throughout her whole life, she was a volunteer and a leader in her community and church. She was a Scouter, true-blue and devoted, and she worked tirelessly for more than thirty years in the Boy Scout organization helping young boys become men. She was involved in her community groups and civic clubs, and, once her kids were grown, she literally spent most of her time involved in volunteer work.

A few years ago, Millie died suddenly on her way to the National Boy Scout Jamboree where she was to receive an award for her service. I attended her funeral where there was standing room only as one person after another saluted this woman. And there in the paper was her obituary: "Millie, dedicated volunteer and Scout leader." Now *that's* a great life.

Millie's life was full of lessons, but one of my favorites was this: Don't wait. She didn't wait to get involved. She didn't wait until she had enough money. (She had none.) She didn't wait until she had enough free time. (She had six kids and arguably no free time.) She didn't wait until she'd settled into a new community or made new friends. (She started working as soon as she moved to our neighborhood.) She didn't wait to find the right charity that matched what she wanted to do. Millie did whatever was asked of her—even the humblest of jobs that no one else wanted to do. Don't wait to give; Millie didn't.

Look Out the Window

I remember when I was in college. School was hard, and I was always broke. I had no free time. I wasn't dating. I was really bummed out and depressed. So I wrote my dad a letter. I seem to recall it was an extremely lengthy epistle filled with "Woe is me! My life is the pits!" I catalogued all my complaints and problems and went on and on about how depressed I was.

About a week or so later, I received an envelope in the mail. It was from my dad. I was really excited because my dad almost never wrote. I eagerly opened the envelope and found a 3x5 card with a message written in big bold print: "Stop looking in the mirror and start looking out the window. Love, Dad."

I was furious. Absolutely furious. Hadn't he been listening? Didn't he read my letter? Didn't he care? Where was the loving, supportive dad I *needed*? This was so like my simplistic father. All he ever thought about was helping other people. Didn't he realize that sometimes I was the one who needed some help?

I had been helping others all my life—my dad had raised us to do that. But didn't *I* deserve some attention once in a while? I stewed for quite a long time. After about a month, I grew up a bit and faced facts. The truth was that my concerns and problems were miniscule in the big scheme of things. Not dating paled in the face of my sister going through a divorce. Homework was nothing compared to those yearning for an education but unable to afford one.

I started to look out the window and to reach out to others, and, as I did so, an amazing thing happened (as it always does): I changed. My problems shrank and most went away completely. My dad's note on that 3x5 card was the best advice he has ever given me.

Start looking out the window. Be aware of others. Don't wait; decide to give. These are life-changing practices.

Do Good and Be Good

We have been counseled to get involved and to do good. President Gordon B. Hinckley stated,

> You are good. But it is not enough just to be good. You must be good for something. You must contribute good to the world. The world must be a better place for your presence. And the good that is in you must be spread to others. . . . In this world so filled with problems, so constantly threatened by dark and evil challenges, you can and must rise above mediocrity, above indifference. You can become involved and speak with a strong voice for that which is right.[2]

Why have we been counseled to get involved? Because we have the truth. Because we have the Spirit. Because we can make a difference. And because, in the Church, we're well-trained by constant service!

But thinking of doing good and serving others often feels overwhelming. We immediately think of all of our responsibilities, projects, commitments, and to-do lists, and we can stop before we even begin. We worry that we can't add one more thing to our lives, and we wonder how we can balance it all without dropping it all! But perhaps there is a way to serve that won't burn us out or do us in.

To begin, we must choose to live our lives as givers. Now I'm not recommending that you quit your job and join the Peace Corps. What I am recommending is that you take a stand right here, right now, in your life and choose to be a giver. And I mean for this decision to extend beyond your family, your closest group of friends, and your ward. I am hoping that you will take a chance to set your mind in a new way and stretch a little. I want you to look at life as a giver would.

Being a giver can be as simple as saying in our minds "I will be a giver." It needn't be a complex list of to-do's or should-do's. We can begin by establishing an outward-focusing spirit. We can decide that we'll be a person who gives—in a variety of ways and in a variety of settings.

Little Moments

As we make the choice to be a giver, it is helpful to look at the best example we have of a person who chose to live the life of a giver: Jesus Christ. As we examine His life, something interesting emerges.

The story of the life of Jesus is filled with what I call little moments. Jesus had all power; He could have literally waved His hand and healed the masses. But He didn't. Instead, His entire life was filled with little moments—one-on-one personal contact. Think about that.

The Savior touched the eyes of the blind man and healed him. He held the children one by one on His lap. With His hand, He raised a palsied man from his couch. He taught not only groups of people but the individual as well. Why did He do all that?

I believe He lived His life that way for us. He ministered to people one by one so we could see how it is done. He taught the greatest lessons by His example, and His example may not have been quite as powerful to us as individuals if He had used His power to heal everyone at once.

In our own way, we have the power to do what Christ did. We have the power to serve in little moments every day. How long does it take to pat your teenager on the back and say, "I'm proud of you, son"? A split second. How long does it take to smile at the grocery clerk? A split second. How long does it take to tell your assistant that she did a great job? A split second.

That split second of service can be an amazing gift for you and for others. Indeed, Jesus told us clearly that we are to follow His example: "Verily, verily, I say unto you, this is my gospel; and ye know the things that ye must do in my church; for the works which ye have seen me do that shall ye also do; for that which ye have seen me do even that shall ye do" (3 Nephi 27:21).

Now clearly, we may not be called upon to heal the leper or raise the dead, but we can do His works. His works were to minister to the needs of those around him, moment by moment, person by person. We can do that. His works are to spread love and kindness and care and teaching. We can do that.

So how do we go about it? I would like to suggest a little experiment. Decide right now that you will give away five split seconds a day. Raise your hand and repeat after me: "I, [fill in your name], pledge to give away five split seconds a day."

Now, imagine your morning. You remember your pledge and begin looking for opportunities to give away your split seconds. Perhaps you say to your spouse or roommate, "Wow, you are looking fantastic today!" How will their day begin then? They'll be off to work or school with their head held high and a smile on their face!

You go into your nursery and hug and kiss your baby. Oh, the smiles you get! One split second of joy to start the day.

You don't stop there. You poke your head into your teenager's room and exclaim, "Hey, sweetheart, I just want you to know I think you rock!" (OK, your teen might be seriously startled over that so pick your own positive comment.)

You go to the family dog and rub his head and ears. Oh, the tail-wagging that will ensue from that one second of attention. You're on a roll now! You head out on the freeway and smile and wave at the person trying to merge and let them in.

By now you're smiling, you're singing, you're feeling so happy you're amazed. And every person (or animal!) whose life you touched for a second is having a happy, joyful day because you gave them a split second of love and attention. It cost you nothing, and it took almost no time at all.

Now I have to warn you, giving away split seconds becomes rather addictive and contagious. Five seconds will feel so good that you'll decide that just for today, you'll try to give away *ten* split seconds. You'll be spreading smiles and love through the grocery store, at the PTA meeting, and around your office. That wave of love will have an enormous impact as it ripples out from you everywhere you go. Can you see the power of living this way?

As you choose to live as a giver, every day will be transformed and you will find yourself doing the works that Jesus did, moment by moment. As you consciously make an effort to serve, you will find changes occurring in the way you think. You'll find yourself noticing others more and seizing opportunities to extend love. You'll find yourself *thinking* more like the Savior as you choose to *act* more like the Savior.

Five split seconds. An easy way to live our life as a giver. All it takes is one decision and a few moments of our time.

But making the decision is crucial. It is that choice that drives the behavior that follows. Making the choice to be a giver sets us on the path of charity. Those few moments of service can change our minds and begin to create in us a charitable heart that leads to even more charity. President Henry B. Eyring described it well:

It was King Benjamin who said to his people, "Learn that when ye are in the service of your fellow beings ye are . . . in the service of your God." [Mosiah 2:17.] And it was Mormon who taught in his words in the Book of Mormon, "Charity is the pure love of Christ, and it endureth forever; and whoso is found possessed of it at the last day, it shall be well with him." [Moroni 7:47.]

The Lord is keeping His promise to you as you keep yours. As you serve others for Him, He lets you feel His love. And in time, feelings of charity become part of your very nature. And you will receive the assurance of Mormon in your heart as you persist in serving others in life that all will be well with you.[3]

A Lesson in CPR

My friend shared a story with me that profoundly affected my outlook on this idea. She had been at the beach one day and she saw a man come out of the ocean holding what appeared to be a rag doll. He laid it down in the sand and stood over it. Curious, my friend walked over to investigate.

The man turned to her and said, "I thought this was a doll rubbing up against my legs in the surf, but when I picked it up, I realized it was a little girl." Horrified, my friend looked down at the body of a toddler.

"What should we do?" the man asked.

"I don't know," replied my friend. Soon several others had gathered and they all stood around the child, all asking what should be done.

Now let's pause and ask a question. Did these people *care* about the child? Of course they did!

Now the next question: Did that *help* the child? No, alas, caring alone did not!

Another man came up to the group, saw the toddler in the sand, and announced, "I'll go get a lifeguard!" Off he ran. The lifeguard arrived, performed CPR, and saved the child's life.

I now think of CPR in a much different way:

CPR = Caring Plus Response

It is not always enough to just *care*. To actually help someone, we must respond in some way to those feelings of empathy.

The Savior taught through His teachings and His actions that it is the response that makes a difference. My very favorite scripture is Matthew 25:40:

And the King shall answer and say unto them, Verily I say unto you, Inasmuch as ye have done it unto one of the least of these my brethren, ye have done it unto me.

Christ taught many powerful lessons in this verse, beginning with the truth that He wants each of us to serve. "Inasmuch as *ye* have done it"—ponder that statement. Why does the Lord want us to serve? There is, of course, the element of providing a benefit to the needy person, which is a wonderful thing, but there is another element that is equally important to Him and that is what service does to us.

Service makes us more like Christ. It increases our charity and our love for others. It increases our understanding of the human family because as we serve, our relationships with our spiritual brothers and sisters grow and expand. Service can also put our own lives and trials in perspective. The Lord is concerned about *both* parties in the service equation, and *both* parties—those who give and those who receive—are blessed.

President Henry B. Eyring tells of a time when the thought came to him, "Everything I have that's good is a gift from God. How would he have me use my gifts to serve someone?" He then asked his wife, who was busy with many tasks, if he could help. She asked him to make the bed, which he did. He then reflected,

> It was such a small thing that I'm sure it doesn't sound very impressive to you, and it probably wasn't very impressive to her either. . . . But as I did that simple little thing, I felt something that I've felt before. When I gave of my time in a way I thought the Savior would want me to for my wife, not only did my love for her increase—I also felt *his* love for her.
>
> I promise you that if you'll use your gifts to serve someone else, you'll feel the Lord's love for that person. You'll also feel his love for you.[4]

This is that "caring" part of the "CPR." As you serve, you will feel His love flowing both ways.

The Lord's instruction continues in Matthew 25:40 as He says, "Inasmuch as ye *have done it*" (emphasis added). The Lord tells us that the action is important. We are to take action on our feelings.

So not only does

CPR = Caring Plus Response

But we can also remember His counsel the same way:

CPR = Christ Pointed the Route!

Our actions can be big or small. Abinadi managed to convert only one person in King Noah's court, and he didn't even know that he had succeeded in that! And yet that one conversion led to the conversion of thousands. The Lord doesn't always ask that we do only great, large acts of service. He just asks that we do something. Do some good. Even if it takes only a split second. Start there and watch where it leads. We may never know the power or the impact of that one small action that took us only a moment.

Make It Personal—for You and for Them

I love the Savior's phrase "unto the least of these my brethren" (Matthew 25:40). What a tender teaching. We are to serve everyone we encounter, even those who we might consider "the least." My aunt used to say that every person is wearing an invisible sign that says, "Please make me feel important!" Indeed Christ teaches us to make our service personal. He reached out over and over to everyone—the unpopular, the social pariah, the different. Each person received His attention. We, too, can be personal in our work.

Moroni says, in talking of our day, "Why do ye adorn yourselves with that which hath no life, and yet suffer the hungry, and the needy, and the naked, and the sick and the afflicted to pass by you, and *notice them not*?" (Mormon 8:39; emphasis added). Where is our focus? Are we noticing those around us who could use our attention?

Not only can we strive to be personal in our good works but we can and should teach our children to do so as well. I was driving with my young son one day, and he saw a homeless man with his boy standing on the median strip asking for help. Tanner wanted to help so we drove to a McDonald's restaurant and he bought a meal for the man and a Happy Meal for the little boy. We drove back, and he handed the food to the man and his son. The man was thrilled and told Tanner that his little boy had wanted a Happy Meal but he couldn't afford it. Tanner was so happy to help. How much more personal was this experience for my son and this man than if Mom had just handed over five bucks? The personal touch blessed all of us.

One mother helped her children establish a tradition of service at Christmastime. She would let the children look through the store catalogs to pick out their Christmas gifts but would also include charity catalogs as well. The children were thrilled with being able to "buy" an animal for a village in need. The first year, the family considered buying a camera phone for themselves, but decided to "purchase" a cow from one of the charities instead. They kept a picture of the cow and named it "Camera Phone." The next few years they "purchased" goats that they named Sega Genesis I and Sega Genesis II. The children loved to donate because they were able to see the pictures of the people who needed their help.

The mother then related, "We need to teach our children that all people on the globe are more alike than different. We need to tell them that we are blessed with a great bounty we can share, that we can make a difference. Children are practical. We fear that they will worry and feel sad when shown the world's greatest needs, but much more often their response is action. They love to help. People in need are helped, human bonds are forged, children grow up with hearts more giving and more open. And every family should know the joy of owning its very own cow."[5]

Christ concludes the verse in Matthew with this glorious statement: "Inasmuch as ye have done it unto one of the least of these my brethren, ye have done it unto me" (25:40).

What a privilege it is to serve others and to serve Him!

Why Serve?

My son once asked me, "Mom, why do you do so much community service?" At first I was concerned that perhaps he felt I was spending too much time in those pursuits, but then I realized what he really wanted to know was "why?" What was my motivation?

I pondered for a while because I felt his question deserved a serious answer. I realized what it was that inspired me to serve, and I told him, "Honey, the Savior did something for me and for my children that I could not do for myself. He atoned for me and for you. I owe Him everything. With all that He has done for me and for my family, how could I not serve? I do it because I love my Savior."

The reason that I find the scripture in Matthew to be so thrilling is that in it the Lord is instructing us all on how we can in some very tiny way, give something back to Him. Every time we help, every time we are kind, every time we relieve suffering we have done it unto Him—Him who has saved us all.

And we can start today by giving away five split seconds of love!

CHAPTER 2

Standing Up

"But rise, and stand upon thy feet."
—ACTS 26:16

I grew up in Michigan where there are a lot of lakes. Consequently, I spent a lot of time in a canoe. Our family had a silver canoe big enough to hold our entire family. The last person to get in was always my grandmother. Grandma was a large woman, and when she sat down in the canoe, we would end up maybe one inch above the water. Finally, in would come the dog. I don't know what possessed us to go canoeing with a dog, but we did.

Buster Browne was a Boston terrier. (He was so much a part of our family that he carried our family's last name.) Whenever we went canoeing, he would sit on Grandma's lap and she would hold the leash, which was critical as Buster would occasionally make a grand attempt at escape, leaping out of the canoe at random moments. Grandma would drag him back in with the leash, and he would end up a sodden mess in her lap.

There was one very big rule while canoeing with the entire family: Do *not* stand up! And you can see why. First of all, we were very close to the water, and second of all, we didn't want to tip the canoe and cause Grandma to fall out. And you knew that if you stood up, everybody else would have to adjust their position to keep the canoe balanced, and nobody wanted to move. Frankly, we were all crammed in there and it was very difficult to move. So that was the rule. Do *not* stand up.

I was reminded of that rule again when my son was in the musical *Guys and Dolls.* In one scene, the group of gamblers and reprobates are at the mission, and a sweet young woman is trying to convince them to repent. Finally, one man has the courage to stand up and confess his sins. All the other men are upset and begin to sing, "Sit down, sit down, sit down, sit down! Sit down you're rocking the boat!" None of the men wanted him to confess because they didn't want to feel guilty themselves and have to do something about it.

The world gives us these same messages over and over: Sit down! Keep the status quo. Don't raise your hand. Don't speak up. Don't volunteer. Do *not* rock the boat! That message is everywhere—at work, at school, even sometimes at church.

But it's not God's message.

"The Mists of Darkness"

Lehi's dream that is recounted in the Book of Mormon describes the works of Satan as "an exceedingly great mist of darkness" (1 Nephi 8:23; see also 1 Nephi 12:17). That word *mist* is a powerful description. If things suddenly turn pitch-black and dark, we would notice and do something about it. But mist tends to overcome us gradually and slowly until we find ourselves lost and blind. Satan will use the tactics of apathy, numbness, and fear to keep us from being aware of those things and people around us that need our attention. We must not succumb to the mists of darkness.

Apathy and the Status Quo

It's human nature to resist change. *We* resist change! Change is scary! It's messy! It's hard!

And the status quo is safe. It's easier. We want to keep things familiar and safe.

But promoting the status quo is also one of Satan's tactics. The scriptures speak of his efforts to keep us apathetic and stationary:

> And others will he pacify, and lull them away into carnal security, that they will say: All is well in Zion; yea, Zion prospereth, all is well—and thus the devil cheateth their souls, and leadeth them away carefully down to hell.
>
> And behold, others he flattereth away, and telleth them there is no hell; and he saith unto them: I am no devil, for there is none—and thus he whispereth in their ears, until he grasps them with his awful chains, from whence there is no deliverance. . . .
>
> Therefore, wo be unto him that is at ease in Zion!
>
> Wo be unto him that crieth: All is well! (2 Nephi 28:21–22, 24–25)

Satan loves for us to stay sitting down. He loves for us to keep our heads down and our hands down. If he can keep us clamped down, he can keep our spirits down. This is definitely one of Satan's more effective tactics.

Helen Keller said, "Science may have found a cure for most evils; but it has found no remedy for the worst of them all—the apathy of human beings."[1]

Apathy is dangerous. Apathy keeps us in the status quo.

Numbed and Dulled Senses

Added to apathy, Satan desires to anesthetize our world. I've had five surgeries due to breast cancer and I have to say I always loved having that meeting with my anesthesiologist prior to surgery. In my appointments, they would ask if I had handled anesthesia well in the past. Oh, yeah, I love it!

Why do I love it? Well, when I'm under anesthesia, *I don't feel anything*—no pain, no discomfort, nada! For surgery, that's pretty important.

But in life, it is dangerous. Satan is trying to anesthetize us so we won't *feel* anything. He wants to neutralize our desires and numb our senses so we don't feel those promptings to stand up, let alone actually *do* something!

Fear

Another tactic used by the adversary is that of feeding our fears. So we have these thoughts:

- "What will the neighbors think?"
- "What if people laugh at me?"
- "What would that do to my family? My reputation?"
- "What if I mess up?"

Such scary things! Satan finds that spark of fear, and then he and his buddies throw on the lighter fluid and fan the flames.

If he can keep us scared, *we will not act.*

We'll run and hide.

Satan may encourage us to hide, but President Gordon B. Hinckley encouraged us in the opposite direction: "You can be a leader. You *must* be a leader . . . in those causes for which the Church stands. . . . The adversary of all truth would put into your heart a reluctance to make an effort. Cast that fear aside and be valiant in the cause of truth and righteousness."[2]

18

A Call to Action

There are so many things in this world that need fixing! So many people to help! Consider this short list:

- Family values (marriage between a man and a woman, number of children) are under attack and being redefined by law.
- Countries around the world face the loss of political freedom.
- Many people suffer under the financial bondage of debt, struggle with poverty, or face unemployment.
- Violence is everywhere in our society (terrorist attacks, suicide bombers, kidnappings, spouse and child abuse).
- Media outlets (movies, music, books, and the Internet) continue to push the envelope of what many people consider to be acceptable.
- Moral issues are being debated and justified (the question of abortion, the need for chastity and fidelity).
- Many people are addicted to drugs, alcohol, or pornography.
- AIDS and other diseases affect people and families around the world.
- The widowed and the fatherless need help and support.
- Immodesty and inappropriate physical appearance (tattoos, piercings) are increasingly on display.

The list could go on, but that seems like a pretty impressive start!

President Gordon B. Hinckley, in one of his finest addresses ever, in my opinion, issued a prophetic call to action. He said, "I believe the challenge to oppose this evil is one from which members of The Church of Jesus Christ of Latter-day Saints, as citizens, *cannot shrink*."[3] We cannot shrink from the challenge to oppose evil. It's truly the latter days, and we signed up for hard-ship duty!

Don't you feel tired and overwhelmed just thinking about it all? I know I definitely feel the urge to sit down! Actually, I feel the need to lie down and pull the covers over my head!

So what are we doing about these things? If the answer is nothing, why not?

Mothers Without Borders and the AIDS Crisis

I grew up in Detroit and I live in Southern California, but it wasn't until I traveled to Africa with the Mothers Without Borders organization that I truly understood the scope of the AIDS crisis. I went to the countries of Zambia and Zimbabwe. Almost one-third of Zambia is dying from AIDS and other serious illnesses. Throughout much of Africa, AIDS and its related illnesses is a scourge that is killing millions. Seeing for myself the effects of the disease—especially on the children—was overwhelming and transforming.

I saw poverty, malaria and other diseases, and ignorance, but the effect of AIDS was the most sobering. I saw so many children living on the streets or with a grandmother who had taken them in. I saw children dying; I watched a newborn baby die, so sick from birth. I saw cemeteries full of AIDS victims.

How could I have been content to go through my life in sunny California and not be aware of what was happening in the world? How could I *not* do something?

I thought to myself, "If a third of Americans were dying, the entire world would pay attention and be galvanized to action. And yet a decimating scourge is here in these countries and the world is paying very little attention."

But what can we do? How can we do it? Even after I went to Africa, I found it easy to slip back into my life and forget.

I remember the first time I went to Walmart after I visited

Africa. I wept. I stood in the doorway with tears running down my cheeks because I looked at the store through the eyes of an African woman. I realized that there was enough food and supplies in that single store to help villages and villages of people.

But now, I don't think about it very much. I shop at Walmart and go back to my usual life. Fear and apathy's tentacles are quiet and constant.

Doing Good Things

In addition to dealing with the bad things that need fixing, there's also a long list of *good things* that need doing!

- Literacy programs to support
- Quilts to sew
- Houses to build
- Children to teach
- Elderly to care for
- Good laws to get passed
- Kits to be assembled (Good heavens! There are *lots* of kits to be assembled!)

So what are we doing about these good things? If the answer is nothing—again, why not? Here the reason is often busyness!

Elder Dallin H. Oaks once gave a wonderful talk entitled "Good, Better, Best" that encourages us to seek to do the "best."[4] And we must remember that "doing good" is often the very "best" thing we can do.

So what can we do? I'd like to share with you some ideas and hope that the Spirit will direct you to your own individual response that is appropriate to you and your circumstances.

Embrace Your Unique Destiny

We must stand for truth and righteousness. As the Lord counseled Paul, "Rise, and stand upon thy feet" (Acts 26:16). In a world that would have us sit down, we can and we must stand up!

To give us courage, we need to recognize who we are and what our mission is. "The Family: A Proclamation to the World" speaks in clear language of our mission:

> All human beings—male and female—are created in the image of God. Each is a beloved spirit son or daughter of heavenly parents, and, as such, *each has a divine nature and destiny.*[5]

It doesn't say *most,* or *some,* or just those who can sing well or dance or organize. It says that *each one* of us has our own individual divine nature and our own individual destiny.

Each of us was sent here at this time, at this place, with a particular mission to perform. Elder James J. Hamula of the Seventy said this:

> To ensure its ultimate success, the final restoration of God's kingdom has been commenced with unprecedented spiritual power and is being sustained by that same spiritual power and something more. Reserved to come forth in these last days and labor for our Father and His Son are some of the most valiant and noble of our Father's sons and daughters. Their valiance and nobility were demonstrated in the pre-earth struggle with Satan. There, "being left to choose good or evil," they "[chose] good" and exhibited "exceedingly great faith" and "good works." Such are the traits that are now needed to sustain the work of God in the earth and to save the souls of men from the intensifying wrath of the adversary.[6]

You are covenant royalty of God. You have been saved until these last days. Do you think that everyone else was valiant and you were accidently slipped in because you were left over? I don't think so!

You were sent to earth at this time because you were among the most faithful, the most committed, the most intelligent, the most capable. The best of the best. The noble and great. That is who you were and that is who you *are*!

Gandhi said, "The difference between what we do and what we are capable of doing would suffice to solve most of the world's problems."[7]

Can you catch a glimpse of the greatness of which you are capable?

You are the celestial ones. Never, ever lose sight of who you really are. You have great power. Do not waste it!

Discover Your Life's Mission

So what is your mission? The answer is something each of us must learn and discover. I would encourage you to make it a daily quest to receive the Lord's direction on this matter. Realize, though, that the answer will be different for each of us and it may grow and change as we respond to the Lord's promptings with willingness. As we repeatedly say, "I am willing" and take those first steps forward, the Lord will guide us and help us discover our true mission in life.

I had an unusually personal experience with this a few years ago. I had been asked to be the regional coordinator for Proposition 8 in California. (Prop 8 was the effort in our state to pass a constitutional amendment to protect traditional marriage.) As part of my duties, I was asked to speak at a rally fireside to kick off our efforts. I was sitting in front of a group of more than two thousand people, reviewing in my mind what I was going to say to all those people.

As I sat there, my vision was expanded. It was very strange. It was as if my vision multiplied and multiplied until I was seeing tens of thousands of people. As I saw this, the Spirit communicated to me very directly that I had done this before—that in the premortal life I had spoken in support of Heavenly Father's plan for the salvation of His family. I had encouraged my premortal brothers and sisters to be strong and to choose to accept Father's plan.

And I knew in that moment that I had been sent here again for the same purpose—to boldly stand and defend God's plan of salvation of the human family. I knew that was part of my mission.

I was fifty years old at the time. As I look back over my life, I can see that I had been prepared for a very long time to perform this mission.

Your mission will be your own.

Perhaps it is to be a valiant youth who can influence others in high school.

Perhaps it is to be a faithful temple worker.

Perhaps it is to be a bold and strong mother.

Perhaps it is to run for public office and change a community.

Perhaps it is to make hundreds of hats for children in South America.

Perhaps it is to write a single letter to the editor testifying of truth and swaying public opinion.

What is *your* mission? Ask Heavenly Father and He will tell you. He will tell you bit by bit as you ask and as you act on the answers. I believe He is just waiting for us to ask! Then He can identify for us the next steps we should take.

"Stand . . . in All Places"

We live in the latter days. It is a world of darkness where people wander aimlessly, lost.

President Gordon B. Hinckley, in describing our day, said,

We live in a day of shifting values, of changing standards, of will-o'-the-wisp programs that blossom in the morning and die in the evening. We see this in government, we see it in public and private morality, we see it in the homes of the people, we see it in the churches, and we even see it among some of our own members who are led away by the sophistry of men.

Men everywhere seem to be groping as in darkness, casting aside the traditions that were the strength of our society yet unable to find a new star to guide them.[8]

That is so true, and it feels like things are getting darker still.

In the latter days, we will need to have strong voices for truth. In the Book of Mormon, Alma called the people to be baptized and asked them if they were willing "to stand as witnesses of God at all times and in all things, and in all places" (Mosiah 18:9). I love that verse. It doesn't limit us to talking only to our friends, only in our church, only in safe places. It boldly calls us to stand in *all places*.

The Lord adds His call to us. In Doctrine and Covenants 27:16, He says, "Stand, therefore, having your loins girt about with truth, having on the breastplate of righteousness, and your feet shod with the preparation of the gospel of peace, which I have sent mine angels to commit unto you." Once again, we are challenged to stand up!

Are we willing to stand? Or are we sitting in the back hoping no one will notice us?

I want to share with you a story about my mother. When I was about fifteen, my family lived in Detroit, Michigan. One day my mother read in the newspaper that there was going to be a lecture given at a local church. It was the largest church in our community with more than 4,500 members. The article said that the lecture was going to "expose the Mormon cult."

My mother said, "I think I'll go."

My brother and I were horrified. "Please don't go!" we said. "You'll embarrass us! Lots of our friends go to that church. Please don't go."

This decision was so not like my mom. She was fairly quiet and reserved so we thought that would be the end of it. Oh, no! She went to the meeting and sat right in the middle of the congregation. For an hour and a half, the pastor read all kinds of anti-Mormon literature, bashed the Church, and told all kinds of lies. Finally, he stopped and asked, "Are there any questions?"

At this point, my mother raised her hand. He called on her, and she stood resolutely—all five feet four inches of her—and said, "I am a member of The Church of Jesus Christ of Latter-day Saints, which you call the Mormons. I categorically deny everything you have said as lies and falsehoods. If anyone would like to know the truth about The Church of Jesus Christ of Latter-day Saints, I would be happy to answer their questions. I'll wait in the foyer afterward."

And she sat down.

At this point, the pastor turned white and the entire congregation began to study their shoes. They were mortified. No one else had any questions.

And then it was like the parting of the Red Sea as my mother walked through the congregation to the foyer and stood as thousands of people walked past her in embarrassment and shame, knowing that they had heard lies that day.

My mom came home and told us what she had done. We were stunned! She had never done anything like that in her life. She had gotten out of her comfort zone, responded to a prompting to do something completely unlike anything she had ever done before, and was able to testify of truth to thousands. I have never been prouder of my mother than I was in that moment.

Elder M. Russell Ballard states:

> Standing for truth and right is not solely a Sunday thing. Every day our neighborhoods and communities are in desperate need of our support and our commitment. . . .
>
> If we are not careful, today's secret combinations can obtain power and influence just as quickly and just as completely as they did in Book of Mormon times.[9]

He is right. There are secret combinations that surround us. Some we are aware of but do not realize what they truly are; others we are unaware of entirely. Evil forces abound.

President Gordon B. Hinckley also spoke of our responsibility to stand up and fight:

> I am one who believes that we should earnestly and sincerely and positively express our convictions to those given the heavy responsibility of making and enforcing our laws. The sad fact is that the minority who call for greater liberalization, who peddle and devour pornography, who encourage and feed on licentious display make their voices heard until those in our legislatures may come to believe that what they say represents the will of the majority. We are not likely to get that which we do not speak up for.
>
> Let our voices be heard. I hope they will not be shrill voices, but I hope we shall speak with such conviction that those to whom we speak shall know of the strength of our feeling and the sincerity of our effort. Remarkable consequences often flow from a well-written letter and a postage stamp. Remarkable results come of quiet conversation with those who carry heavy responsibilities.

Declared the Lord to this people:

"Wherefore, be not weary in well-doing, for ye are

laying the foundation of a great work. And out of small things proceedeth that which is great.

"Behold, the Lord requireth the heart and a willing mind" (D&C 64:33–34).

This is the essence of the matter—"the heart and a willing mind." . . .

I think the Lord would say to us, "Rise, and stand upon thy feet, and speak up for truth and goodness and decency and virtue."[10]

A Single Voice Can Make a Difference

I currently serve on the city council in my community. One e-mail, one letter, one visit from a person can have an enormous influence. I don't think people realize how much power of influence they have. And it doesn't matter how old they are—I receive e-mails from children and teenagers all the time, and they have significant impact.

So often we feel tired or discouraged and think that the country is sinking and there's nothing we can do about it. Satan delights in this kind of thinking! He's the one telling us to be discouraged and to sit down. But, as our prophet has said, remarkable results come as we take small, collective steps for action.

Those steps can be big or small. We can be old or young. Every step makes a difference. Every voice is important. I'd like to share two experiences, remarkable in their similarities, that illustrate that truth.

Justin

Many years ago, I was attending a city council meeting. I was sitting in the back when in came our Scout troop to work on their Citizenship in the Community merit badge. They had certainly picked an interesting meeting to attend! The primary item on the agenda was the consideration of an application by a tattoo parlor that wanted to come to our small town.

I listened in dismay as one speaker after another spoke glowingly about the need for new businesses to come to town and how we needed to support this application. When the head of the chamber of commerce also spoke in favor of the business, the boys in the Scout troop were shocked. The man was LDS, and in Southern California that was uncommon, so I know the Scouts had hoped he, at least, would oppose the application.

One boy in particular was very agitated. Justin was "that boy" in the troop. You know the type. He was a rascal. He was a smart boy, but sometimes he had trouble controlling himself. You never knew what he was going to do. Well, Justin was upset about the meeting. Then he got mad. He kept squirming in his seat and loudly whispering, "Sister Boyack! I want to speak. Can I speak? Come on, let me speak." I resisted because, well, who knew what he would say?

Finally, I thought, *What could it hurt?* So I told him to take a speaker's slip up to the clerk. Soon they called his name, and Justin walked up with his shirt untucked, wild hair, and a scowl on his face. He stood at the microphone.

"How old are you, Justin?" asked the mayor.

"I'm twelve years old," responded Justin.

"Go ahead then," replied the mayor.

And then Justin let them have it.

"This is nuts!" he fairly shouted. "I walk my little sisters to school right past this plaza. Lots of us walk past there to go to school. We shouldn't have a business like this there. It's wrong! Everyone knows that this city is for families. That's what's important. This business is bad for families. You shouldn't let it come here. I don't care what anyone else has said—*this is wrong*!"

And then he walked with clenched fists back to his seat.

When it was time for the council members to speak, one after another echoed Justin: "This does not belong in our community." And they voted it down.

It was the only time I had ever seen a business voted down, and all because of a twelve-year-old boy who stood up and let his voice be heard.

Josh

I once received a phone call from a school board member asking for my help. A parent was challenging the school district because he was an atheist and did not want the Pledge of Allegiance to be recited in school with the phrase "under God" included. He was also demanding that the district provide a "God-free" classroom for his daughter where no mention of God would ever be made and no discussion of any religion would be offered. The school board member asked me to help spread the word so that they would have some support in the board meeting to be held the next day. I agreed to help and sent out an e-mail to a few thousand of my close, personal friends.

When I arrived at the meeting the next evening, I had to sit in the back because the room was already packed with hundreds of people and lots of television cameras. I asked a mother how it was going. "Oh, it's going OK," she replied. "I'm surprised at how many people are supporting the guy."

At that point, the clerk called out, "And next we have a slip from Josh Carpenter, opposed to the request, and not wishing to speak."

The woman's son jerked his head up. "Mom, they called my name!" She turned to her son and tried to quiet him, assuring him that they had said he was opposed. He was crestfallen. "I know . . . but, Mom, I really wanted to speak."

Well, I had seen what Justin had done in another meeting so I turned to the mother. "He must speak! He absolutely must speak!"

Josh smiled, but his mother was a bit startled. She asked, "What should I do?"

I told her to fill out another speaker's slip and run it up to the clerk and tell the clerk that Josh definitely wanted to speak. A short while later, the clerk called Josh's name.

When Josh walked up in front of those hundreds of people and all those cameras, the board president looked at him and asked, "How old are you?"

"I'm twelve years old," he replied. (I just love fearless twelve-year-old boys!)

The president said he could speak—and Josh did!

"I don't understand this at all," said Josh. "We live in America! This just isn't right. I have five friends: one is Buddhist, one is Catholic, one is Muslim, one is Jewish, and I'm Mormon. We all get along just fine. Some of us stand for the pledge, some of us don't. Some say 'under God' and some don't. That's OK. We're in America.

"If you have to have a separate classroom for the atheists, then you'd have to have a separate classroom for the Buddhists and one for the Catholics and one for the Muslims. That isn't right! That isn't the way this country is. We came to America to have freedom of religion so that we could all worship any way we want. We can all live together peacefully. That's how we do things in America!"

The whole place erupted into a standing ovation for this twelve-year-old boy.

At the end of the meeting, many of the school board members quoted Josh and said, "Josh is right. This is America." And they rejected the proposal.

One person—even one child—can change a community!

CHAPTER 3

Withstand Evil

*"Wherefore take unto you the whole armour of God,
that ye may be able to withstand in the evil day,
and having done all, to stand."*

—EPHESIANS 6:13

The Lord is counting on us to withstand evil. The latter days are ripe with evil, but often we don't really realize it until we think back to the past. As I see things in the news or in the media, I realize that we would never have seen those things ten or fifteen years ago. What was once abhorrent is now acceptable, even desirable, and it's getting worse.

We have many opportunities to stand for truth and be a witness of God. It's up to us to be the one to speak against evil. President Gordon B. Hinckley said,

Stand up for integrity in your business, in your profession, in your home, in the society of which you are a part.

Again, it is not enough that you retreat to your private cloister and pursue only your special private interests. Your strong voice is needed. The weight of your stance may be enough to tip the scales in the direction of truth.[1]

One voice can make a difference. One person speaking up can influence and lead others.

One day my son came home from high school and informed me that he had had a rather strange day. It was called the "Day of Silence," and it was a new "activity" sponsored by a club at school that supported an alternative lifestyle. On this day, everyone was encouraged to wear buttons and not speak as a way to show support for the members of this club who felt that they did not have a voice to speak. My son's science teacher began the class by handing out buttons to everyone (my son politely declined) and then stood in front of the class but didn't speak for the entire hour.

I called the principal the next day to find out exactly what had happened. He said that there was nothing that could be done about it because it was a club activity.

Nothing could be done? Wrong answer.

I served on the PTA (which is a great way to get involved), and the next day we had a meeting. I didn't know the rest of the parents because I was new, but the principal was there. I spoke up.

I described what had happened at the school and then said, "I don't know how all of you feel about this, but it is wrong. This activity disrupted an entire school day. It brought to the day a topic that is private. The teachers are paid to teach—not promote their own, or someone else's, agenda. It should never happen again."

I held my breath. And then, one after another, each parent spoke against the activity and supported my position. By the time we got to the principal, he was squirming and said he would look into it.

One voice. The weight of one person's stance tipped the scales.

I wish I could say that we were able to completely eliminate the activity, but we were able to at least get the district to require that teachers teach during school hours and not distribute anything. We were also able to get the club's activities limited to after-school hours. But the battle continues.

The next year, I wrote an opinion editorial for the local paper regarding the Day of Silence. I said that schools were for teaching, not for spreading political agendas or discussing private behavior. Oh, my. The newspaper got responses for many months as the battle raged back and forth.

Parents became much more aware of what was going on at the school, and they began to respond. So the second year many of us kept our children out of school for the day and called the school district to tell them our reason. The school district was shocked. Awareness continued to grow. Policies were reviewed. The battle continues.

One voice. The weight of one person's stance tipped the scales.

I have heard it said that all that is necessary for evil to triumph is for good men to do nothing.

Each of us can do *something*. And that may be enough.

May I issue a call to each of you?

Commit today to be one of those who can always be counted on to *stand up* and *speak up*.

This is no small commitment. But it is a commitment we can and must make. We were sent here for this very purpose.

This may be overwhelming to some people, if not most, so how do we make that commitment? Where do we begin?

Respond to Promptings

We can once again begin with the Lord. The Lord will guide us to those times when we need to stand up. He did that with my mother, He did that with Justin and Josh, and He did that with me. Each of us received a prompting to stand up and speak up, and we responded.

That is it in a nutshell. We will receive promptings from time to time that encourage us to stand up against evil. What we do about those promptings is up to us. We can reject them out of fear. We can ignore them out of apathy. Or we can respond to them with courage and faith. It is as simple as that.

Once we make the commitment to be one of those who can be counted on, then we must begin to listen. We can pray each day to be directed in the things we experience and encounter so we know when our voice is needed. We can choose to respond to the promptings that come.

The choice is pretty basic. "I choose to respond to promptings that come to me to stand up and speak up." There. Seems simple enough.

Face Our "Days of Decision"

Ah, but sometimes when the promptings come, they are not always easy. Our resolve and our faithfulness will be tested.

President Gordon B. Hinckley referred to these moments as "days of decision." He states, "There may be times of discouragement and deep concern. There certainly will be days of decision in the lives of each of us. It was ever thus."[2]

In an earlier address, he had encouraged all of us to rise to excellence:

This is the great day of decision for each of us. For many it is the time of beginning something that will go on for as long as you live. I plead with you: don't be a scrub! Rise to the high ground of spiritual, mental, and physical excellence. You can do it. You may not be a genius. You may be lacking in some skills. But so many of us can do better than we are now doing. We are members of this great Church whose influence is now felt over the world. We are people with a present and with a future. Don't muff your opportunities. Be excellent.[3]

We face many days of decision. We can choose to step up and speak up and rise to reach our higher abilities of excellence. Or we can "be a scrub." The choice, as always, is ours and ours alone.

A few years ago, the mayor of our city passed away and the council needed to appoint a new mayor. I was being considered for the position when a young woman from our community stood and spoke to the council. She railed against me because of my involvement in Proposition 8, claiming that I could not represent the city. She acknowledged that I had helped many people in the community, including her own family, but stated that my opinions on traditional marriage made me unfit for the position of mayor.

I sat there listening and wanted to point out that all of the other council members, including the other person being considered for the appointment, had also supported Proposition 8. I was about to speak when the Spirit constrained me. Very quietly I heard, "Merrilee, do not speak. This is *their* day of decision." I sat quietly—which is hard for me to do!—and there was great silence. Not one of the other council members spoke up to defend Proposition 8, to declare their position, or to defend me. There was only the silence.

During our days of decision, sometimes we will prevail and sometimes we will fail, but the point is that we must try.

Stand with Moral Courage

It is that first step—that choice to stand up—that is critical. President Thomas S. Monson encouraged us with these words:

As we go about living from day to day, it is almost inevitable that our faith will be challenged. We may at times find ourselves surrounded by others and yet standing in the minority or even standing alone concerning what is acceptable and what is not. Do we have the moral courage to stand firm for our beliefs, even if by so doing we must stand alone? As holders of the priesthood of God, it is essential that we are able to face—with courage—whatever challenges come our way.[4]

This applies to all of us. We must each stand with moral courage. We must choose to respond to promptings in those days of decision.

So what can we do?

- E-mail or call your political representatives regularly about the issues you are passionate about. Be respectful but firm in your message.
- Vote in every election.
- Visit your children's schools and pay attention to the curriculum. Read what your children read. Be involved in their classrooms and with their teachers. Let the teachers know your standards and ask them to alert you if anything comes up that may violate those standards.
- Develop an e-mail list of like-minded individuals. Communicate with those on your list about issues that are important to you or about opportunities for service.
- Write a Facebook or blog post or tweet about something you believe in.
- Attend and speak at your local meetings. Anyone can speak about anything at the beginning of these public meetings, so use that time to change things!

I have listed even more suggestions to consider in the Appendix, but I believe it comes down to two simple things:

When we hear or see or read something evil—we can take action.

When we feel a prompting—we can take action. We can literally ask the question, "What is it that I should do?" If we ask that, we will be guided to what it is we can do.

Elder Richard G. Scott issued this call:

> . . . There is an urgent need for more men and women like you who will stand for principles against growing pressures to compromise. Men and women are needed who will act nobly and courageously for what the Lord has defined as right—not for what is politically correct or socially acceptable. . . . You can be an essential part of that shining light, that righteous influence to increase the moral fiber of this nation and its homes.[5]

If we do not speak up, who will?

If we do not act courageously, who will?

If the Lord cannot count on us to *stand for truth,* whom can He count on?

Once we express a willingness to the Lord that we will stand up and speak up, promptings will come to us. As we respond to those promptings by taking action, a couple of interesting things will happen.

First, it will get easier! We will gain confidence. Indeed, our confidence in the Lord will wax stronger and we will become braver and not worry so much about what other people think.

Second, it will get harder. I know that sounds odd. But the Lord needs valiant servants and once we step up to be one, He will call on us more and more. But through it all, He will be with us. President Thomas S. Monson urged us, "Do not pray for tasks equal to your abilities, but pray for abilities equal to your tasks.

Then the performance of your tasks will be no miracle, but you will be the miracle."[6]

Defend Our Families against Evil

As we stand against evil, we must also defend our families against evil. Our battle starts there.

Pornography is pernicious and pervasive, and it is wreaking havoc on personal lives, marriages, and families. It is a cancer that is spreading and growing and devouring families, leaving sorrow and heartache in its wake. Immoral sexual activity of all kinds is also spreading and growing.

Our families are not immune. Our marriages are not immune. Satan is at war, and the sooner we realize that we, too, are at war for our very souls, the better.

I once received a letter from a concerned mother that describes this battle well. She wrote:

> I just need to take a moment and thank you so much. I went to your series of talks during Education Week and what an eye-opener! We always think that our children are for the most part good people, but Satan is much, much bigger and more enticing.
>
> After listening to you, I began to listen more to my children. I mean really listen. . . . I did notice my daughter spending much, much more time on our computer. . . . One day someone had mentioned to my husband to check out [a social media site] and look for our daughter. [The mother then relates all the troubling things she and her husband found on their daughter's account and on her friends' accounts.]
>
> What is so sad is that a lot of our youth who come from great active homes are on [this site] too doing the same thing.

I guess why I am sending this to you is so that maybe during your lectures you could inform parents of this site. It is awful. It is evil. It is BIG. I opened my own account (with a false name, of course) so that I could do the research on my daughter and her friends. Within 30 seconds, I had someone send me a message with a filthy little innuendo in it. Satan really is a hard worker and wants to steal the innocence and beauty of our children. He has nestled himself in a perfect battle position.[7]

Satan's war is gaining momentum. So as we stand up for truth, we must stand for our families as well.

We must protect our children.

We must protect our marriages.

We must protect our families.

That requires us to be very vigilant. We cannot assume that all is well or that we are safe.

One of the things I encourage parents to do is to read everything their children read first. I also encourage them to go into the school classrooms and pay attention.

Vicky is a mother of several children. One day, her eleven-year-old son came home from school with a pamphlet that had been handed out. She read it and was shocked at its contents. It was a sex education pamphlet that described all kinds of sexual activities in graphic detail, including deviant behavior. She immediately spoke with both the teacher and the principal, but was told that there was nothing they could do, that they were required to teach the material.

Nothing they could do? Wrong answer.

Vicky had tried to go through the proper channels, but now it was time to try another way. She went to the school board meeting and stood up to speak.

She said, "Let me read to you from a pamphlet that was given to my eleven-year-old child." And she began to read these graphic descriptions from the pamphlet. The school board was shocked! They protested, "Oh, no, please stop."

She said, "Oh, no. You've sent this home with my eleven-year-old child. Let me read some more." And she did.

The board was horrified and protested vehemently. "Please, please stop. We will investigate this immediately."

The school board eventually learned that the pamphlet had been sent directly to three different middle schools in the district from an alternative lifestyle organization. *It had not come from the school district at all!* The school district was completely unaware that this had occurred.

Not only that, but this pamphlet and its offensive material had been taught in the schools for *three years.*

For three years, children had been taught and instructed in deviant behavior by their teachers—all because no mother, no father, had looked at the material and objected. The school district immediately implemented safeguards to prevent anything like that from ever happening again. All because one mother paid attention and spoke up.

That one mother protected her family, her children, and many other children. That lone warning voice was enough.

We must pray and seek help to protect our family from evil. The Spirit will warn us. I remember many times our sons commenting, "How do you guys know when we mess up?" I told them that the Spirit was screaming at us, warning us when they were slipping. We, as parents, are entitled to that protection for our children, and we can ask for it.

But we must be aware. We must watch ever so carefully and be vigilant.

Stay Vigilant

Recently, I was sitting with some clients in my living room (I work at home), and one client mentioned that I had bees swarming outside my window. He was right! Bees were swarming around the outside wall and chimney of our home. We called our pest control buddy and asked him what we should do.

He informed us that the allure of a queen bee was tremendous. She could be "smelled" by other bees from up to three miles away! He also told us that even if the queen was dead, she could still be smelled and the bees would still come. The only way to get the bees to leave was to remove the queen bee completely and then carefully seal all possible openings.

Now there were a couple of ways of doing this. One required that we rip out a huge section of our living room wall, remove all the bees, treat the area, and then restore it. This would be an extremely expensive option.

Then he said, "There is a second way, but most homeowners won't do it." He said that we could hook up a vacuum to the area, seal it with tape, and suck the bees out. This option sounded much cheaper! "But," he cautioned, "this takes a long time. You have to be constantly vigilant. And you have to persist until you get the queen out."

"How will we know when the queen is out?" we asked.

"The bees will stop coming," he replied.

The process took several weeks. Every night, my husband carefully checked the area to see if bees were moving in or out. He would check the big pile of "processed" (i.e., dead) bees to look for the queen. Eventually, everything finally seemed clear and we were happy. But we kept the hose hooked up just in case.

It's a good thing we did, because after a couple of bee-free weeks, they came back. We began again to run the vacuum and check the bees for the queen. I must admit that I was getting tired of that vacuum running! I urged my husband to just have professionals handle it. But he persisted.

Finally, we could see no more bees. It's been a year now, and we are still bee-free. My husband squirted bleach in the openings to counteract the smell of the queen bee, then filled the openings with expanding foam and sealed them all carefully. But we stay aware of the danger, just in case they return.

This experience reminds me greatly of the spiritual and moral perils that face our families and our homes. Temptation is swarming all around us and trying to get into our homes. Most of us want a quick fix. Most of us want someone else to deal with it.

Like the queen bee, there is often one temptation that provides the greatest attraction. We have to remove that temptation through repentance and stay vigilant that it does not return. We must constantly remove evil from our lives through daily repentance, and we must encourage our children to do the same.

Then, while we get things under control, we must do a thorough cleansing, both spiritually and environmentally, filling our lives with good things so that there is no room for evil to return. And we must never forget that we are in danger. We must take action, and we must be constantly vigilant. And we must never, ever stop.

One way to cleanse our home's environment is to literally remove evil influences. Go through your home and look for signs that evil is getting in. Are there movies, books, magazines, or video games with questionable content? Do we have clothes that are suggestive? Is the computer unprotected by passwords or filters? On and on we go, cleansing and protecting our homes. And sometimes we think we're clear for a while, but if we are not vigilant, those evil influences can creep back in.

I recommend getting a giant garbage can and putting it right in the middle of the family room and have a family home evening where you gather items from your home that are not uplifting or appropriate and chuck them in! Then celebrate by replacing them with celestial things in your home to keep it clean!

We also need to be vigilant with our computers. I cannot advocate strongly enough the importance of having filtering software on our computers to protect each other and our children. My husband has installed software on our computers that limits the amount of time our children are online. When their time is up, the computer automatically shuts down. We can also set the level of filtering to block access to any objectionable material.

It also allows us to monitor all the websites our children visit, which has provided some amusing experiences. One day my husband was on a business trip in New York, and he called me in the middle of the day. "Somebody is looking at bikinis!" he stated.

"What?" I asked in confusion.

"On the computer," he explained. "Somebody just looked at a website with bikinis. Go check it out."

Only one of my sons was home at the time, so I went into the family room, where we keep our home computer.

"Son, were you looking at bikinis on the computer?" I asked.

He looked at me, and his eyes bugged out. "What are you talking about?" he stalled.

"Dad called from New York and said that someone was looking at bikinis on the computer. You're the only one home."

Duly busted, he admitted that he had looked—only briefly, of course—at a website on the computer. We were able to have a good discussion about how such behaviors led to worse behaviors, and he was contrite.

One little bee had been sniffing around our home. Luckily, my husband had been paying attention.

President Thomas S. Monson warns us,

> To an alarming extent, our children today are being educated by the media, including the Internet. . . . It is our

responsibility not only to teach them to be sound in spirit and doctrine but also to help them stay that way, regardless of the outside forces they may encounter. This will require much time and effort on our part—and in order to help others, we ourselves need the spiritual and moral courage to withstand the evil we see on every side.[8]

In a wonderful talk given to the fathers of young women, Elaine S. Dalton, Young Women general president, issued a call:

Fathers, you are the guardians of your homes, your wives, and your children. Today, "it is not an easy thing to protect one's family against intrusions of evil into [their] minds and spirits. . . . These influences can and do flow freely into the home. Satan [is very clever]. He need not break down the door."

You must be the guardians of virtue. "A priesthood holder is *virtuous*. Virtuous behavior implies that [you have] pure thoughts and clean actions. . . . Virtue is . . . an attribute of godliness." It "is akin to holiness." The Young Women values are Christlike attributes which include the value of virtue. We now call upon you to join with us in leading the world in a return to virtue. In order to do so, you "must practise virtue and holiness" [D&C 46:33] by eliminating from your life anything that is evil and inconsistent with one who holds the holy priesthood of God. "Let virtue garnish thy thoughts unceasingly; then shall thy confidence wax strong in the presence of God; and . . . the Holy Ghost shall be thy constant companion." [D&C 121:36.][9]

I believe that call is to all of us—not just fathers. Each of us must be guardians of virtue. We must begin in our own lives, and then we must extend our efforts to those around us.

Lead Others to Withstand Evil

As we take action when we see, hear, or read evil, others will notice. As we take action to protect our families, others will ask questions. We have a great opportunity to lead others to withstand the evil influences all around us.

President Thomas S. Monson said, "You are a mighty force for good, one of the most powerful in the entire world. Your influence ranges far beyond yourself and your home and touches others all around the globe."[10] We can extend our influence beyond our own circle as we reach out to others. Others are waiting for us; they are willing to help—they just don't know where to start.

One of my practices as a mother is to pre-read the books and assignments that are given to my children to make sure the material is acceptable. I have shared this practice with other parents in my area, and one day I received a call from a mother who was alarmed by the book her fourth-grade child had been assigned to read for class. She had decided to read the book first and was horrified by the content, which contained several intense situations. She had contacted the teacher, who was fairly unsympathetic to her concerns. Eventually, the mother was able to get the principal to intervene, and the teacher assigned her child another book.

"But what about all the other children?" she asked me. "What about all the children in the district?" We discussed the situation, and I decided to go meet with the officials at the school district. I learned all about how books and curriculum were selected, and then I asked if parents could have input in this process. The school district officials welcomed the suggestion.

Over the years, I have been collecting e-mail addresses of parents who shared similar values, and we called ourselves The Informed Parents Group. When issues would arise in our schools, we would notify each other and use our collective influence to change things that needed to be changed.

So I took this challenge regarding the assigned reading to our group. The parents agreed to each read books for their child's grade level. Working together, we were able to review a large number of books and succeeded in having some books removed entirely from the curriculum and others moved up to more mature grade levels as appropriate. We tried to be very cooperative and positive with the school district, and they, in turn, were very cooperative with us.

This group of parents grew and grew and became a major source of influence within the district. And it started with one e-mail to the people I knew asking if they wanted to unite, share information, and take action.

Just a Mom from Gilbert, Arizona

As we unite, we can have tremendous influence on others and withstand much evil around us. I was once speaking on the topic of standing up against evil and afterward I was approached by a couple of women who said, "Oh, you have to meet our sister!" That's how I met Sharon Slater.

Sharon grew up in California. She graduated from Brigham Young University with a degree in family sciences. She served a mission in Costa Rica and Panama, and then married her husband, Gregory, who was a convert. They settled in Gilbert, Arizona, to raise a family.

Sharon had four children and was a happy, stay-at-home mom. She had never been involved in anything political, not even PTA. When her youngest child started kindergarten, Sharon found she had time on her hands. She started playing tennis, but that lasted only about a month. She thought, *What am I doing?*

This is not why I am here on earth. She began praying and asking Heavenly Father what she should be doing with her time.

A few months later, her husband forwarded to her an e-mail from Richard Wilkins, a BYU law professor who had gone to the United Nations and found many major assaults on the family occurring there. "The Family: A Proclamation to the World" had recently been given, and Brother Wilkins used that document to deliver a speech to a large group at the UN. The e-mail contained this sentence: "Who knows but that the Proclamation on the Family was given for such a time as this?"

"I felt impacted at a very deep level when I read that sentence. It moved me and I felt the Spirit very strongly," Sharon said. She found out that there was a woman in her ward who had been at the UN when Richard Wilkins had delivered his speech. The woman was now trying to raise money to attend a conference at the UN.

A few weeks later, Sharon was sitting in a Relief Society class when the teacher posed a question: "How can we be a voice to the nations of the world?" That riveted her attention. Her hand shot up and she said, "We can raise money to help this woman in our ward so she can go to the UN!" A few women said they would help, and soon Sharon was organizing a fundraiser to help the woman in her ward and her husband go to the World Congress of Families.

The night before the fundraiser, Sharon woke up in the middle of the night with the thought that she was supposed to start an organization to help promote the family. She thought of three goals:

1. Educate people about the threats to the family.
2. Organize them to protect the family.
3. Mobilize them to action.

She said, "Then the thought came to me that if I was going to lead the organization, I needed training because I knew nothing.

Maybe I should go to the World Congress [which was only a few days away]. I called my husband who was in China on a business trip and said we needed to go. He said, 'Let's do it!'"

She and her husband went to the World Congress conference and learned all about the threats to the family at the international level. Sharon was invited by another organization to attend a UN conference a few months later, which she planned to do. The night before the meeting, she felt impressed to study a book with family-related provisions from UN documents and to highlight some of the paragraphs.

The next day in the meeting, a UN delegate was trying to defend the family and was under attack. Sharon began shaking when she realized that the paragraphs she had highlighted the night before were the very references the delegate needed to defend her position. Very discreetly, she got the booklet from her bag, opened it to the right page, and slipped it into the delegate's hands. When the delegate saw it, she used the references and prevailed.

The delegate cornered her afterward and asked, "Who are you?"

"I'm just a mom from Gilbert, Arizona," Sharon replied.

When Sharon told me this story, she added, "I was a mom who happened to be in the right place at the right time with the right tool. If a mom with no experience could have an impact on international relations, what could many of us, united, do?" She began to bring teams to the UN negotiations and has since had hundreds of experiences where international policy was affected.

While Sharon was attending a UN Conference in South Africa, she felt impressed that she should visit Mozambique while she was there. She wanted to see about implementing an abstinence-based HIV/AIDS program that she had helped develop through her friend's organization in Mozambique. When her guide picked her and her husband up at the airport, she felt that she should ask him if he had any brothers or sisters. He said that he had three in the same orphanage that they had planned to visit.

The thought immediately came to her that she was supposed to adopt them. She dismissed the idea as crazy. The HIV/AIDS program was reaching more than a million children in thirteen countries. Why should she adopt those children when she could help so many more?

She said, "As I was introduced to the children, I tried to avoid them. Their mom and dad had died of AIDS, and they had other siblings there. It didn't seem logical to take them away from this brother who clearly cared about them. I continued to push away the thoughts about adopting them until an hour before I was to leave. I mentioned to a volunteer that I had had these thoughts, and the woman looked at me and said, 'I can't tell you how right that is.' At that moment I felt like Heavenly Father had taken a 2x4 to my head. 'Hello! These thoughts are not your thoughts. You are supposed to adopt these children!' I was in shock. But, I had made a commitment to follow through on whatever the Lord asked me to do. I immediately found my husband and told him that I thought we were supposed to adopt these children. After he recovered from the shock, he asked, 'What do you want me to do?' I asked him to talk to the older brother while I waited in the car that was to take us back to the airport.

"We didn't find out until later that the older brother had joined the Church and had baptized these children shortly before we got there. He wanted to go on a mission, and he had been praying for a family to come and adopt his siblings so he could go and not have to worry about leaving his family behind in the orphanage. Later, he went on his mission but due to health reasons had to come home early. He was honorably released and soon thereafter died of AIDS."[11]

Seven years later, after much adversity, Sharon and her husband were able to adopt those three children. The oldest two have both played a miraculous role in speaking before the United Nations conferences in the defense of families.

Sharon Slater has written *Stand for the Family* and is now the president of Family Watch International with members in 170 countries. (You can learn more about the organization at FamilyWatchInternational.org.) They work to protect the family worldwide. Sharon is leading people worldwide in pledging to Stand for the Family. (You can sign that pledge and join the movement at StandfortheFamily.org.)

Sharon was enlightened by the Spirit every step of the way, and her journey has led her along paths she would have never dreamed of.

We can walk with the Spirit and look for light and guidance in all that we do. We can respond to the Spirit's promptings. We can ignore Satan's messages of hopelessness and darkness. We can seek enlightenment every day. We can covenant with our Heavenly Father that we will do what He asks, no matter what. Then we can pray each day and listen and respond to the promptings that will come. They may be big, or they may be small. But day after day, we can strive to respond and to lead others.

We can do this. Let others know what you're doing. Ask what they think. Focus on positive solutions. Then we can truly be a mighty force for good as we withstand evil together.

CHAPTER 4

Rich in Good Works

"That they do good, that they be rich in good works,
ready to distribute, willing to communicate."

—1 TIMOTHY 6:18

Not only must we be actively working against evil, but we must also be active in building up the kingdom of God. We must be building Zion—and that does not just mean in the Church—that means in the world.

President Howard W. Hunter said,

> We entreat you to minister with your powerful influence for good in strengthening our families, our church, and our communities.
>
> We recognize that much good comes from individuals and organizations who reach out to remedy the ills of the world. We encourage you to follow the scriptural admonition to be anxiously engaged or actively involved in good causes in the Church and in your neighborhoods, communities, and even throughout the world. (See D&C 58:27.) . . .
>
> Those who follow Christ seek to follow his example. His suffering on behalf of our sins, shortcomings, sorrows,

and sicknesses should motivate us to similarly reach out in charity and compassion to those around us.[1]

We can each take steps to work toward doing good. As I mentioned, it starts with a choice. The Primary song "I Will Be Valiant" reminds us of this choice and ends with the declaration: "The Lord can depend on me."[2]

What a wonderful attitude! We have made covenants to remember those in need and to help them, and we also have made covenants to take upon us the name of Jesus and, in so doing, we commit to do His work.

When we think of doing good in the world, we might wonder where to start and what to do.

I always start with God. Just ask Him. As President Gordon B. Hinckley reminded us: "Let us be prayerful. Let us pray for righteousness. Let us pray for the forces of good. Let us reach out to help men and women of goodwill, whatever their religious persuasion and wherever they live. Let us stand firm against evil, both at home and abroad."[3] Prayer is an excellent first step. We can then be open to the promptings that will come.

In order to stay in tune with the mind and will of the Lord, we can live our lives in a way that will foster a spirit of charity and goodness. There are several steps we can take.

Alma, in the Book of Mormon, offered this unique perspective on helping others.

> Yea, he saw great inequality among the people, some lifting themselves up with their pride, despising others, turning their backs upon the needy and the naked and those who were hungry, and those who were athirst, and those who were sick and afflicted.
>
> Now this was a great cause for lamentations among the people, while others were abasing themselves, succoring those who stood in need of their succor, such as

imparting their substance to the poor and the needy, feeding the hungry, and suffering all manner of afflictions, for Christ's sake, who should come according to the spirit of prophecy. (Alma 4:12)

There is great need in the world, some seen and some unseen. But the Lord is aware of it all. He sees it all. One way we can help others is to see as He sees.

Open Our Eyes

Recently I went to the Brigham Young University art museum to see an exhibit of work by Carl Bloch, a renowned Danish artist from the late 1800s. The artwork was magnificent to see, but I found myself drawn to one painting in particular. There were benches in front of the painting, and so I sat down to ponder the scene.

The painting was of Christ standing by the pool at Bethesda. Do you remember the story?

Now there is at Jerusalem by the sheep market a pool, which is called in the Hebrew tongue Bethesda, having five porches.

In these lay a great multitude of impotent folk, of blind, halt, withered, waiting for the moving of the water.

For an angel went down at a certain season into the pool, and troubled the water: whosoever then first after the troubling of the water stepped in was made whole of whatsoever disease he had.

And a certain man was there, which had an infirmity thirty and eight years.

When Jesus saw him lie, and knew that he had been now a long time in that case, he saith unto him, Wilt thou be made whole?

The impotent man answered him, Sir, I have no man, when the water is troubled, to put me into the pool: but while I am coming, another steppeth down before me.

Jesus saith unto him, Rise, take up thy bed, and walk.

And immediately the man was made whole, and took up his bed, and walked: and on the same day was the sabbath. (John 5:2–9)

It's a beautiful story of healing, and Carl Bloch's depiction of it is compelling.

In the painting, the Savior is standing to the left of center. He glows with light and love. To the right are the people who are waiting beside the pool and need healing—a woman, a child, a man. In the center is the infirm man who could not walk. In the painting, this man is in shadow, under a tattered awning; he is gaunt and withered. Behind Jesus to the left are His disciples. They are turned away, not looking at those in need.

And then you notice the focal point of the painting. Christ is lifting the awning and looking directly at the withered man. A tiny bit of light can be seen in the man's eyes as the light from the Savior reaches his face. There is a look of tenderness and compassion in Jesus' face. And there is a look of questioning amazement in the man's expression.

You can just tell that no one had ever looked at him like that. No one had paid any attention to him. No one had ever noticed his need. Everyone looked away.

Except Him. He who had the power to heal saw His brother in need, and He healed him.

Another story of Christ teaches this principle as well.

. . . Jesus therefore, being wearied with his journey, sat thus on [Jacob's] well: and it was about the sixth hour.

There cometh a woman of Samaria to draw water: Jesus saith unto her, Give me to drink.

(For his disciples were gone away unto the city to buy meat.)

Then saith the woman of Samaria unto him, How is it that thou, being a Jew, askest drink of me, which am a woman of Samaria? for the Jews have no dealings with the Samaritans. . . .

And upon this came his disciples, and marvelled that he talked with the woman: yet no man said, What seekest thou? or, Why talkest thou with her? . . .

And many of the Samaritans of that city believed on him for the saying of the woman, which testified, He told me all that ever I did.

So when the Samaritans were come unto him, they besought him that he would tarry with them: and he abode there two days.

And many more believed because of his own word;

And said unto the woman, Now we believe, not because of thy saying: for we have heard him ourselves, and know that this is indeed the Christ, the Saviour of the world. (John 4:6–9, 27, 39–42)

The disciples marveled that Christ would talk to a woman—and a Samaritan woman at that. They could not fathom such a thing. But Christ was different.

He saw the woman. He talked to her. And in so doing, converted her, and she in turn helped to convert many through her testimony.

Sometimes we find ourselves not looking. We avert our eyes so we don't look at the homeless man, the disabled woman, the person who is suffering.

As we try to become disciples of Christ, we learn the importance of not looking away. We must learn to *see* the needy, to *see* the poor, and to *see* the needs of those around us.

Do we have eyes that see?

My sister Andrea drives to work every day on the freeway and every day she goes under a particular underpass. One day she looked to the side and realized that there were people under the underpass. She was startled. The next day, she looked more closely. It wasn't just a group of people—it was a family.

She couldn't believe what she was seeing and quickly pulled over. The family was standing near a garbage can, warming their hands over a fire. She went to talk to them, and they said they had no place to live. Andrea asked, "What do you need?" They said they were hungry. So she drove home, gathered up a large box of food, and brought it back.

This began a regular practice of my sister and her family taking food to the homeless. Her family even developed a tradition of making two Thanksgiving dinners—one for the homeless, which they deliver first, and then one for their family that they eat later, grateful for their blessings.

A disciple of Christ sees.

Lettie is such a disciple. Lettie lives in Harare, the capital of Zimbabwe. One day she was walking down a street and heard children crying. She stopped and looked into a doorway and saw five little children. "What are you doing?" she asked. "Why are you crying?"

One child spoke up. "Our mother has died, and our father is dead. We are all alone."

"Where are your people?" asked Lettie. In Africa, extended families often take care of the children if they can.

The children told her they were from Mozambique and that their parents had come to Zimbabwe for work, but now they were alone.

Lettie took the children home and fed them. She told them to come back the next day and she would feed them again. They returned the next day and the next. And then they told some other children and more came. Word began to spread among the other orphans and street children.

Lettie went to the churches in the area and asked for help and a few people responded.

I met Lettie in 2006 when I went to visit her with Kathy Headlee Miner, the founder of Mothers Without Borders. (Visit MothersWithoutBorders.org for information about this program.) I sat in Lettie's tiny backyard and watched as half a dozen adults cooked over open fires and more than two hundred children lined up to be fed. The children took their plates of food and sat on the patio in the front yard. After they had eaten, Lettie and her friends led the children in reciting scripture and poetry, singing songs of Jesus, and dancing. When they were done and hugs had been exchanged, the children happily filed out to the street, full of food for another day.

One woman had eyes to see. One woman stopped and looked.

I think we sometimes don't realize the power of that small step—the power of just looking around us and noticing others. In that moment when we see, we see our sister or our brother; we don't see "that person who is different." We see our family. And it is in that moment that the Lord can prompt us and tell us how we can help.

Kathy Headlee Miner tells of an experience she had many years ago when her children were young. She had taken her family to a fast-food restaurant for lunch and was trying to ride herd on all of them. She realized that her little daughter, whom she was holding, was smiling and waving at the man behind her, who was obviously a homeless man. Kathy stopped her daughter from waving and settled the family at a table. But her little one continued to smile and laugh and wave at the man as he sat at his table. He shyly waved back. This continued for some time even though Kathy was a bit apprehensive about the attention.

When the man had finished his meal, he hesitantly approached

Kathy. "I just want to thank you," he said. "Your little daughter has brought me such joy. No one looks at me or smiles at me. So I really appreciate your little one being so friendly."

Kathy was surprised and somewhat chastened. She had been averting her gaze while her innocent little one saw a person to love. A powerful lesson.

Open Our Ears

As we open our eyes to see, we can also open our ears to hear. We can listen for the needs of others as they are not always apparent.

In the Bible, we can read the story of how Jesus healed a man who was blind from birth. The man was then hauled before the Jewish leaders and grilled about what had happened. He told the truth, but the leaders still cast him out. Jesus' reaction is important:

> Jesus heard that they had cast him out; and when he had found him, he said unto him, Dost thou believe on the Son of God?
>
> He answered and said, Who is he, Lord, that I might believe on him?
>
> And Jesus said unto him, Thou hast both seen him, and it is he that talketh with thee.
>
> And he said, Lord, I believe. And he worshipped him. (John 9:35–38)

Jesus was listening—he *heard*—and then He acted immediately to heal the man's soul as He had healed his eyes.

Recently I was walking through an airport and had to walk all the way to the end of the terminal to reach my gate. When I arrived, I was surprised to see that no one else was there. I asked the nearest attendant where the flight for San Diego was, and she said they had moved it to another gate. Then she said, "I've announced it five times, but I guess I'll keep announcing it." I hadn't heard it at all! I was so preoccupied that my ears were closed!

When we open our ears and really listen, the Spirit can truly communicate with us. We become receptive not only to the still small voice but also to the feelings and promptings that come from the Spirit along with it.

I remember speaking at a Time Out for Women conference in Denver, Colorado. It had been a marvelous event, and I was about halfway through my talk when the whole room went dark. The power had gone out! I was standing on a stage in front of more than eighteen hundred women, and it was pitch-black and the microphone was out. I called out to them to sit quietly for a bit while we figured out what had gone wrong. A woman in the audience had a small flashlight that she gave to me. The producer finally reported to me that the power was out in the whole block and it was time for my booming voice.

I walked into the middle of the audience and I asked if everyone could hear me. The women called back that they could. The room then hushed as the crowd waited to hear the rest of my talk. An electric feeling filled the room as I continued my presentation. The women were still as they listened in the dark. It was an amazing experience as the power of the Spirit filled the room and the women opened their ears to hear. When I announced that my next point was "Be Enlightened," there was a moment of quiet, and then the whole place erupted in laughter. There we were, sitting in the dark and listening to a discussion on enlightenment! It was truly a memorable moment.

Later, during the next speaker's presentation, the power came back on, but by then the women were so tuned in to listening that the power of the experience continued throughout the rest of the event.

Sometimes we have to listen carefully in order to hear the

needs of others that we may miss if we're not tuned in with open ears. A few years ago I was suffering some frightening side effects of an unhealthy interaction between medications I was taking. The side effects affected me not only physically but also psychologically. I felt the most gripping fear I've ever felt in my life. I called my sister and told her I was having a problem. She instantly said, "I'll be right over." She came immediately and sat with me and helped me as I struggled through it.

Her ears were open to hear the need in my voice. She didn't just try to reassure me. She didn't just half-listen and then tell me to hang in there. She could hear that I was in serious need and immediately acted to fill that need.

We've all had that happen. Someone says, "How are you doing?" and, with a clenched smile on our face, we answer, "Oh, I'm fine." And yet we're not fine! We need help! And we are so grateful when someone's ears are open enough to hear beyond our words.

It is also important to open our ears in order to hear the Spirit prompt us to act with charity. Elder Carl B. Cook said, "In order to be guided in life's journey and have the constant companionship of the Holy Ghost, we must have a 'hearing ear' and a 'seeing eye,' both directed upward. [Proverbs 20:12.] We must act on the direction we receive. We must look up and step up. And as we do, I know we will cheer up, for God wants us to be happy."[4]

Open Our Hearts

Most important, we can open our hearts. We can allow our hearts to turn to those around us and, as we allow ourselves to feel, the Spirit can touch our hearts and help us to connect with the love of the Lord.

Again, we turn to the life and teaching and example of the Savior. One of the most poignant accounts in the scriptures is the story of Jesus visiting the Nephites. As we read these verses, we can feel of Christ's heart.

And it came to pass that when Jesus had thus spoken, he cast his eyes round about again on the multitude, and beheld they were in tears, and did look steadfastly upon him as if they would ask him to tarry a little longer with them.

And he said unto them: Behold, my bowels are filled with compassion towards you.

Have ye any that are sick among you? Bring them hither. Have ye any that are lame, or blind, or halt, or maimed, or leprous, or that are withered, or that are deaf, or that are afflicted in any manner? Bring them hither and I will heal them, for I have compassion upon you; my bowels are filled with mercy.

For I perceive that ye desire that I should show unto you what I have done unto your brethren at Jerusalem, for I see that your faith is sufficient that I should heal you.

And it came to pass that when he had thus spoken, all the multitude, with one accord, did go forth with their sick and their afflicted, and their lame, and with their blind, and with their dumb, and with all them that were afflicted in any manner; and he did heal them every one as they were brought forth unto him.

And they did all, both they who had been healed and they who were whole, bow down at his feet, and did worship him; and as many as could come for the multitude did kiss his feet, insomuch that they did bathe his feet with their tears.

And it came to pass that he commanded that their little children should be brought.

So they brought their little children and set them down

upon the ground round about him, and Jesus stood in the midst; and the multitude gave way till they had all been brought unto him. . . .

. . . And he said unto them: Blessed are ye because of your faith. And now behold, my joy is full.

And when he had said these words, he wept, and the multitude bare record of it, and he took their little children, one by one, and blessed them, and prayed unto the Father for them.

And when he had done this he wept again;

And he spake unto the multitude, and said unto them: Behold your little ones.

And as they looked to behold they cast their eyes towards heaven, and they saw the heavens open, and they saw angels descending out of heaven as it were in the midst of fire; and they came down and encircled those little ones about, and they were encircled about with fire; and the angels did minister unto them.

And the multitude did see and hear and bear record; and they know that their record is true for they all of them did see and hear, every man for himself; and they were in number about two thousand and five hundred souls; and they did consist of men, women, and children. (3 Nephi 17:5–12, 20–25)

Oh, what a wonderful example of love and tender compassion from the Savior. I cannot imagine what it would have been like to look upon Him as He wept from the power of His great love. His tender care for those who were suffering—and His great love for each little child—tells of a great heart thrown wide open to those around Him.

We can look to His example. We can learn to open our hearts, even if it's only a little bit at first. We can seek to have a heart like Jesus.

When I went to Africa with Mothers Without Borders, we visited a village in the bush country of Zambia. We went there to work with the children and the women. I was walking along a path to another part of the village to teach the children, and soon five little boys had gathered to walk along with me. (I have four sons and I think they just knew a boy-mommy when they saw one!)

We were holding hands, and they were laughing as I sang a funny, nonsensical song to them. They were all orphan boys, wearing dirty, tattered clothing but with such beautiful smiling faces. For a moment, time stood still for me.

My heart opened wide. I looked at each little boy and it was as if their faces were etched upon my heart. I thought, *These are my babies! I have never met them before and I probably will never see them again. But, in this moment, they are my children.* And then I began to feel even more deeply. It was as if I could feel the presence of their mothers and could almost hear them pleading with me, "Please take care of our sons! Please love them." I knew that in that moment, I could love them with a mother's love.

We may be tempted to shield our hearts. Often when we open our hearts to the need around us, we first feel pain and suffering. But then we can quickly move to feeling love and compassion as the Savior did. Opening our hearts is a process and a choice that requires some vulnerability on our part. And sometimes, it takes only a moment.

A few years ago, I was dealing with the challenge of breast cancer, and I was lying facedown in a large MRI machine. I was having a biopsy to check to see if the breast cancer that had been diagnosed was in more than one area. The process was very painful, and the machine was noisy and a little frightening. I had to lie very still for a long time as the machine and the technicians did their job. It was a scary time for me as I wondered what the results would be.

A nurse was standing by me, watching to make sure that I stayed still. During a difficult moment of the procedure, she reached out and touched my hand. She kept her hand on top of mine and would gently and reassuringly pat my hand from time to time.

Oh, I cannot tell you what that small gesture meant to me! I could feel her steady care for me, and it helped me to be able to endure what I had to endure. Her heart had been open, and she had reached out with a tender gesture to calm my sad and troubled heart. I was grateful beyond words.

President Thomas S. Monson speaks of this opening of our hearts as following the example of the Good Shepherd: "Ours is the responsibility to care for the flock, for the precious sheep, these tender lambs, are everywhere to be found—at home in our own families, in the homes of our extended families, and waiting for us in our Church callings. Jesus is our Exemplar. Said He, 'I am the good shepherd, and know my sheep' (John 10:14). We have a shepherding responsibility. May we each step up to serve."[5]

Opening our hearts can be the simple choice to love those around us.

Let me share with you the story of Etta Jean Powell. Etta Jean was born in 1928, and she lived in Detroit, Michigan. She was born with a genetic condition that made it appear as though she had no neck. Etta Jean never married. She lived with her parents until their passing.

Etta Jean was thirty-eight when her life crossed mine. She was my Primary teacher; when I was turning eight years old, she helped me prepare for baptism. I remember she gave me a bookmark listing the Ten Commandments and taught me to be obedient.

What I remember most, though, is that Etta Jean loved me. I absolutely knew that without a doubt. She loved children. She loved people. She taught Primary for decades. Eventually, she taught the grandchildren of some of her first students. She was also a nursery leader for a long time.

She loved to make things for other people; she made the most beautiful quilts and afghans.

Etta Jean never had a driver's license and as a result was always grateful and appreciative of those who drove her around town. She served a mission in the Washington DC Temple. In 2009, Etta Jean Powell died at the age of 81 in Michigan.

Others may look at her life and how humbly she lived and may judge her by that standard alone. But those of us who knew her know better. Etta Jean was meek and humble, and through the challenges she faced, she learned—and shared—powerful lessons about love. She loved each of us. And her life has blessed ours forever.

By the world's standards, her life might be judged as completely unsuccessful. By the Lord's standards, I believe she was stunningly successful. She learned the two things we all came here to learn—to love the Lord with all her heart, might, mind, and strength, and to love her neighbor as herself. She was a woman who lived her life with her heart wide open.

We can follow the Savior's example of love as we open our hearts to those around us. We make the choice to love, and that choice can drive our behavior. In a powerful talk called "When Love Is Why," Russell T. Osguthorpe talks about this choice to love:

> What if our only motive were love? What if everything
> we did, we did out of love? There are all kinds of motives

out there, and many of them are not pretty. We might be motivated by revenge or envy or greed. Selfish motives are abundant. . . .

The Savior's life on earth was short, but He reached out in love every step of the way. He helped so many while He was on His way to help someone else. He noticed what others needed, reached out to them, and helped them— sometimes in simple ways and other times in miraculous ways. Every miracle He performed, every word He spoke, He did out of love. . . .

His life on the earth was an example of what it means to do good. But it was also a singular example of what it means to do good for the right reason. Every act of the Savior on earth was done out of love.[6]

That love can be the driving force we need when we open our hearts to those around us. We can allow those feelings to grow and motivate us to action to care for others as the Savior would have us do.

Pray for Those in Need

Sometimes when we see or hear of a need, there is nothing we can do to help. Sometimes the only thing we can do is pray.

But never underestimate the power of the prayers of the righteous.

There are beautiful and poignant accounts in the scriptures of Jesus praying for others. The account of His visit to the Nephites describes two such instances.

And it came to pass that when they had all been brought, and Jesus stood in the midst, he commanded the multitude that they should kneel down upon the ground.

And it came to pass that when they had knelt upon the

ground, Jesus groaned within himself, and said: Father, I am troubled because of the wickedness of the people of the house of Israel.

And when he had said these words, he himself also knelt upon the earth; and behold he prayed unto the Father, and the things which he prayed cannot be written, and the multitude did bear record who heard him.

And after this manner do they bear record: The eye hath never seen, neither hath the ear heard, before, so great and marvelous things as we saw and heard Jesus speak unto the Father;

And no tongue can speak, neither can there be written by any man, neither can the hearts of men conceive so great and marvelous things as we both saw and heard Jesus speak; and no one can conceive of the joy which filled our souls at the time we heard him pray for us unto the Father.

And it came to pass that when Jesus had made an end of praying unto the Father, he arose; but so great was the joy of the multitude that they were overcome.

And it came to pass that Jesus spake unto them, and bade them arise.

And they arose from the earth, and he said unto them: Blessed are ye because of your faith. And now behold, my joy is full. (3 Nephi 17:13–20)

Jesus returned later and He prayed for them again.

And it came to pass that Jesus departed out of the midst of them, and went a little way off from them and bowed himself to the earth, and he said:

Father, I thank thee that thou hast given the Holy Ghost unto these whom I have chosen; and it is because of their belief in me that I have chosen them out of the world. . . .

And now Father, I pray unto thee for them, and also for all those who shall believe on their words, that they may believe in me, that I may be in them as thou, Father, art in me, that we may be one.

And it came to pass that when Jesus had thus prayed unto the Father, he came unto his disciples, and behold, they did still continue, without ceasing, to pray unto him; and they did not multiply many words, for it was given unto them what they should pray, and they were filled with desire.

And it came to pass that Jesus blessed them as they did pray unto him; and his countenance did smile upon them, and the light of his countenance did shine upon them, and behold they were as white as the countenance and also the garments of Jesus; and behold the whiteness thereof did exceed all the whiteness, yea, even there could be nothing upon earth so white as the whiteness thereof.

And Jesus said unto them: Pray on; nevertheless they did not cease to pray. . . .

And it came to pass that he went again a little way off and prayed unto the Father;

And tongue cannot speak the words which he prayed, neither can be written by man the words which he prayed.

And the multitude did hear and do bear record; and their hearts were open and they did understand in their hearts the words which he prayed.

Nevertheless, so great and marvelous were the words which he prayed that they cannot be written, neither can they be uttered by man. (3 Nephi 19:19–20, 23–26, 31–34)

How marvelous to hear the Savior pray! What power in His prayers! And what was it like to be the beneficiary of His prayers?

We can offer this gift to others. Our prayers can call down the powers of heaven to bless those in need.

When I was a little girl, my mother taught me to pray any time an ambulance went by. We prayed for those who needed the ambulance, and for the paramedics who were helping the injured. When I grew up and had children of my own, I taught them the same thing.

And then the city built a fire station behind our house! The children came to me and said, "Mom, what are we going to do?"

I said, "Kids, we are going to be praying a lot!"

Several times the firefighters have asked me, "Is your family still praying for us?" and I have assured them that we were and always would.

The power of prayer is significant. When I was suffering through breast cancer, I could literally feel the power of the prayers offered by the people in my life. I've never felt that before. It was very, very real, and it truly made a difference in my recovery.

Just imagine the power of hundreds of righteous people combined together in prayer. Being united in prayer makes a difference, and the Lord acknowledges such prayers. But, truly, the prayer of one righteous person can call upon the Lord—and He answers those prayers as well. The prayers of one person can work a miracle.

So when we read in the paper about some distant catastrophe, we can pray. When we drive by an accident, we can pray. When we hear of a sad situation, we can pray. That habit can bring blessings to many and can create in us a love and desire to help others in any way we can.

Contribute Generously

I have seen the power of a simple dollar. It is amazing what one or two dollars can do. When I was in Zimbabwe visiting with the orphans at Lettie's home, I learned that she was feeding the children on two dollars each per *month*. It was incredible to think $400 a month could keep two hundred children alive. I was overwhelmed!

As we met with Lettie and her associates, she said they were asking for a grant of $50 to buy a small machine to make peanut butter so the children could work and make money. Fifty dollars. That's all. I thought, *Wow, I could buy a dress for $50 without a second thought. But to these people, that is a significant amount of money and could generate income for so many.*

That lesson has not been lost on me. Yes, we can work miracles with our generous contributions, but even small amounts of money can make a big difference to those in need.

One time, I was sitting in the drive-through lane of a fast-food restaurant and talking to my youngest son. I said, "Tanner, do you realize that your allowance of $6 could keep three kids alive in Africa? What if the child that you helped grew up and discovered the cure for cancer?" He was so excited by the thought. I talked about how if he saved one child, that child could grow up and be a daddy and provide for his own children and on and on. I said, "Think about that! You could impact generations of people, and you're only six years old!" At that point, Tanner decided we should skip lunch and donate the money instead!

We can also establish family patterns of generosity. We "borrowed" an idea many years ago that has become a wonderful tradition for our family. At Thanksgiving, we give each of our children a pre-paid VISA gift card and ask them to donate the money to someone in need or to a worthy cause. Then, on Christmas evening, we gather to discuss how they donated their money. It is always a sweet time as we listen to the boys share how they felt about helping orphans, supporting an organization for autism, or caring for a person in our ward.

We've also added a birthday gift tradition as well. Our sons are grown so instead of getting them a bunch of birthday presents, we give a KIVA gift certificate. (Visit KIVA.org.) This is a wonderful organization that allows you to make a $25 micro-loan to someone in the world who needs it. You can "shop" through all the requests, which range from a man trying to start a fishing business for his village to a woman wanting to buy a sewing machine to provide for her family, and you can then extend the loan. After the person repays the loan, you receive an e-mail update, and then you can loan the money to someone else! My family loves to participate in this organization and we give these as gift certificates quite regularly to others as well. Truly, small donations can make a huge difference.

One summer I was teaching at BYU Education Week and speaking to the youth on the topic of generosity. I asked the teens, "How many of you have a buck?" Almost everyone raised a hand. Then I asked, "What if each of you donated one dollar to the LDS Humanitarian Fund? You could keep hundreds of children alive this month." The kids seemed rather amazed by this thought.

At the end of my lecture, a young man named Chase ran up and announced, "I'm going to collect everyone's buck!" He grabbed a couple of his buddies and they stood at the doors and held open their backpacks. Hundreds of kids began to throw in money. When the boys were done, they ran over to me to show me backpacks full of money. I was astounded.

"Should we give it to the bishop?" the kids asked. "Or should we give it to you?"

"Give it to the bishop," I said.

"OK," Chase replied. "Should we count it first?"

"By all means," I said. And off they ran to count it.

The next day, Chase approached me at the beginning of class. I asked him to report on what had happened. He stood before the entire group—more than five hundred kids—and told them they had been announcing it and collecting money from all the classes the entire previous day. "We're at $664!" he reported. "Our goal is to hit $1,000 today and donate it all to LDS Humanitarian from the BYU Education Week Class of 2011." We were all stunned! It was incredible what these kids had done!

I encouraged them to continue their efforts. "Imagine if you did this at every youth dance," I said. "What if you all threw in one buck at each dance and donated it?" You could feel the energy run through the room as the teens learned the power of a dollar. They could change the world and save lives through a small contribution multiplied with love.

Many of us are so very blessed with prosperity and our contributions can make a huge difference to people who want to better their lives.

So let's take a pledge! Raise your right hand and repeat after me: "I pledge that I will give up one trip to McDonald's and donate $5 to someone in need this month." Go ahead—you can do it!

Or if you can't do that, how about donating one dollar? The next time you pay your tithing, put one dollar in another category. Just think if one million members donated a dollar each month! The impact would be incredible!

I've done a variety of humanitarian projects over the years, and I've noticed that people react to need in a variety of ways. When a crisis occurs, people have this instinctive desire to give, but they often start with donating used clothes. Truthfully, many people in need mostly need money! They need money to buy food or buy supplies to start a business. The power of that money to change their circumstances is significant.

So choose to contribute. Donate generously as guided by the Spirit. And together we can help people in need.

We can all do these things:

Open our eyes to see those in need around us.

Open our ears to hear the call for help and the promptings of the Spirit.

Open our hearts to feel so that we can respond with love.

Pray for those in need and help use our faith to draw on the powers of heaven.

Contribute generously so that our blessings can bless others.

As we do each of these things, the Lord can guide us to the things He would have us do to bless others. And we will truly be rich in good works.

CHAPTER 5

Do the Greatest Good

"Do the greatest good unto thy fellow beings, and . . .
promote the glory of him who is your Lord."
—DOCTRINE AND COVENANTS 81:4

Responding to those feelings of caring can sometimes be over-whelming. Just the thought of doing good can make you feel like your life is on overload. And it can be challenging to think of what to do and where to start. But "doing good" requires actually *doing* something. It requires action. I hope by now that you have gleaned some ideas on some simple things you could do and simple ways you can begin to help others.

A simple question can help. When we feel caring feelings or hear of someone's need, we can ask, "What should I *do* about this?" And then listen. The answers will come.

Sometimes the answer will be "Just pray." Sometimes the answer will be "Donate!" And sometimes the answer will be "Yes, do this!"

It is important to realize that each of us will do something different in answering that question. We are unique! Our answers can be unique! I think it is liberating to know that we don't have to do the same action somebody else is doing. We can embrace our own unique gifts, skills, and abilities and move confidently in the direction of action that fits us. I believe promptings can come to us based on our abilities and our experiences, even where we live and where we are in our lives. Again, each of us is different. And that is wonderful!

I learned this lesson very dramatically in my community several years ago. We live in the north San Diego area and our city of Poway was severely burned twice by wildfires. After the last wildfire in 2007, I watched this principle of unique, individual action unfold.

I was in Utah speaking about the wildfires of 2004 when my phone began to buzz on the seat behind me. It was the counselor in our stake presidency telling me the fire was approaching our city and our community.

I was serving on the city council at the time, so I flew home immediately. I remember looking out the plane window and seeing wildfires burning uncontrollably all over the area. It was terrifying! I drove quickly to my home and greeted my husband, who was packing our evacuation bags. I knew what I had to do. During the 2004 wildfires, I had run the evacuation center as a volunteer. With this renewed threat, I headed immediately to the evacuation center in our city to help.

My son Tanner was sixteen at the time, and he said, "Mom, I want to go with you!" He had helped in the prior wildfire evacuation. He worked diligently for days and was invaluable in helping the families at the center.

On the third day of the fires, an elderly woman approached me and said, "Merrilee, can you help me? My husband had a massive stroke last week and he's confined to a wheelchair. I haven't been able to clean him. We need help."

I called over my son. "Tanner, this man needs to be bathed and dressed. Can you handle that?"

Time stood still. I saw this young man stand tall and square his shoulders. He said, "Yes, Mom. I can do this." He smiled at the woman and took the handles of her husband's wheelchair and off they went, Tanner chatting with the man who couldn't respond. Tanner took him to the pool building and gently showered him. Then he dressed him in clean clothes and brought him back to his wife. The man was beaming with joy—so happy to be clean again! The woman was in tears and was effusive in her gratitude. "Thank you, thank you so much!" she said.

A couple of years later, I ran into the woman at a volunteer dinner. She said, "Merrilee, do you remember me? Your son bathed my husband during the wildfire." I said that I remembered her and asked how her husband was doing.

"He passed away four days after that," she said. "But he was so happy. I shall never forget the tender love your son showed my husband. It was the most loving thing I've ever seen, and it brought my husband great joy," she said with tears in her eyes.

My son was helping at the center because that was what he felt he should do.

My husband, Steve, is a self-proclaimed nerd. So he received a "nerdy" kind of prompting. A couple of days after the fires hit, he said to me, "I'm feeling so sad for all the teenagers who have lost so much in the fires. People are donating things for young kids and for families, but there is nothing for the teenagers who lost everything they own. I think I'll e-mail Steve Jobs, the CEO of Apple Computers." Now, my husband *loves* Apple Computers. ("Love" is perhaps not a strong enough word. He adores them!) So he wrote an e-mail to Steve Jobs and asked him if Apple would consider donating iPods to the teenagers who had lost their homes in the wildfires. Well, lo and behold, a couple of days later, my husband was contacted by Apple. Steve Jobs had actually read my husband's e-mail! And they wanted to help. My husband was astounded and so happy!

They said, "We would love to do this on one condition—no

media." My husband, of course, promised. And representatives from Apple Computers came to our area and, without fanfare, delivered an iPod to each of the teens we had identified. (Don't tell!) What a precious thing it was for those teenagers.

Another woman was a knitter. She wanted to do something for the thousands of people who had lost everything in the fires. She began to knit and then began to gather other knitters and crocheters, organizing the "San Diego Wildfire Blanket Project." Hundreds joined and created beautiful afghans, quilts, and other lovely homemade items. The families who received those gifts were so touched that complete strangers would take their time to make them something heartfelt and beautiful.

My sister Kathe decided to organize a holiday boutique. She had done something similar in response to the 2004 fires, and since more than four hundred homes had burned in her small community in the 2007 fires, she felt strongly that she wanted to help again.

Kathe is an organizer. So she used her skills and abilities to organize a miracle. She invited community groups from all over the area to participate. We involved the Girl Scouts, churches of all denominations, service clubs, generous individuals—you name it! Countless people drew together to create a miraculous event.

It was so magical as hundreds and hundreds of families who had lost everything came. I remember one man walking into the boutique and just standing there and bursting into tears. It was unbelievable to see so many tables laden with new and gently used items, homemade items, and more. (And every item was *free*.) Thousands of items had been donated. And volunteers were everywhere dispensing lots of hugs and love.

Afterward, I wrote of the experience:

Well, the Holiday Boutique this Saturday was AMAZING, INCREDIBLE, SPLENDIFEROUS, OUTSTANDINGLY FABULISHNESS!!!

I walked in Saturday morning and just stood there STUNNED. My sister, Kathryn, and her team of angels had wrought a MIRACLE. It was HUGE! And such wonderful, beautiful things. Man, oh, man. It was a miracle to behold. I couldn't WAIT for the families to come.

And come they did! And lots of hugs, tears, and discovery unfolded. I cannot tell you all the stories but I'll share some.

One family came in and ran to tell me they had found a ceramic Christmas tree just like the one their grandma had made them.

Another mom, so tired when she went in, just stood there in tears, holding a round tin—just like the one she had before and had used to decorate her kitchen. I could go on and on with the discoveries!

And the kids were GAGA! Oh, it was too wonderful for words.

So thank you to each and every one of you who donated, who worked so hard, and who prayed over this amazing event. God's hand was in this work this day.

And a huge STANDING OVATION from the entire community for my sister, the tireless Kathryn Humberstone, who helped bring another miracle of love and caring to our community. (And let us all pray she does not have to do a THIRD!!! ☺)

It was wonderful to see what one woman with a heart and a specific kind of ability could do.

Gary is a sports fanatic. He loves cycling. So he decided to gather bicycles for the children. Hundreds and hundreds of bicycles and helmets were donated—most were brand-new!—and presented to the kids who had lost their homes and belongings in the fires.

Roger received a musical prompting because he's a musical kind of guy. He realized that all of these kids had lost their musical instruments too. So he organized a drive to collect instruments, both new and used, to help these children.

See how all were prompted in their own unique way according to their gifts, their strengths, and their abilities?

And then there was the little boy in Chicago, Illinois. This ten-year-old boy was watching the news and saw the terrible fires and the homes burning to the ground. He ran into his bedroom and got his new favorite toy that he had just gotten for his birthday. He had his mom help him put it in a box and wrote on the box in his little-boy writing: "To the Firefighters of Poway, California." That box traveled across the country until it reached our firefighters.

They brought it to me and said, "We got this box in the mail and there's a note inside asking that we deliver this to a ten-year-old boy. Do you know one?" I did. Just that day, I had met a family who had lost everything in the fire—and they had a ten-year-old boy.

I took the box to him. He read the note from his new friend in Chicago. The note said, "Hi, I saw the houses burning on TV. That is so sad. But this is my favorite toy that I'm sending to you. It is the coolest Bionicle and it's really hard to find. I hope it makes you happy." The little boy was thrilled with the new toy.

What had prompted a ten-year-old boy to do that? Millions of people had watched that same newscast. Millions of people had felt sad for our community. But one little boy in Chicago, Illinois, jumped up and *did* something! And it blessed a little boy in California and made him happy. One small action had big results for both boys.

The key is to *do* good. Do something! Be it big or small, every single act of goodness contributes light and love to the world. Every single act changes the world.

I've been participating in a little experiment recently. I heard LDS singer Hilary Weeks say that for a long time she would ask in her prayers, "What is the most important thing I should do today?" She would then ponder after her prayer to receive direction.

I was impressed by that and decided to do it as well. Sometimes in my life I feel like I don't do enough. Sometimes I feel like I'm doing way too much! So I decided that would be a worthy exercise for me to let the Lord direct my actions and set my priorities.

It has been an interesting experiment. Some days I receive the most random promptings or ideas. One day I felt I should write a letter of recommendation for a friend who was looking for a job. She hadn't asked me for a letter, but she's an amazing woman so I acted on that prompting. Another day I felt that I should pay attention throughout the day and take the opportunity to show interest in others. One day, when I had a cold, the prompting was distinct—take care of yourself! Rest today. Sometimes we need to show love and caring to ourselves! And another day it was simply to tell my husband that I loved him.

When we let the Lord direct our actions for good and help us prioritize them, then we can know that we are doing the most good at the right time.

But I think it's also perfectly all right for us to do lots of good all on our own. The Lord encourages that!

In the Doctrine and Covenants, we read, "Verily I say, men should be anxiously engaged in a good cause, and do many things of their own free will, and bring to pass much righteousness" (Doctrine and Covenants 58:27).

Those words are inspiring. Notice that the Lord uses the word "should." Not "could" or "may be." Instead He said we all *should* do good. Very clear.

I also love the word "anxiously." One definition says it all: anxiously means "very eager and concerned to do something."[1]

That seems about as far away from passive as you can get! *Very eager* to do good. That mind-set and that passion is encouraged by the Lord.

And then the word "engaged." I am a huge *Star Trek* fan. And as all *Star Trek* fans know, when the captain wants to get the ship moving forward again, he sits up, lifts his right hand, and announces, "Engage!" That's a signal for the helmsman to get moving! When we are engaged in an activity, we are wholly participating. We are sitting up, lifting our hands, and moving forward. We are right in the thick of it.

We should be anxiously engaged in a good cause. Not just an occasional good thing—but in a "good cause." Now that cause may be helping in our families or in the Church. It could include a cause that helps our neighborhood, our community, or the world. I think all of those areas are worthy of our attention! There is so much good to be done and so many places to do it.

And then comes the powerful phrase "do many things of their own free will" (Doctrine and Covenants 58:27). We are to *do*. We're not to just think or wish or care, but we are to do many things. (Notice the Lord says not one but *many*!) And we are to do them of our own free will. The Lord expects us not only to seek direction and be obedient, but He also expects us to come up with good ideas (whether on our own or as a result of seeking direction or inspiration from the Holy Ghost) and to move forward willingly and cheerfully! When we use our caring and our abilities and tap into our will, we can do great things.

And the Lord explains why. When we act on those ideas and those feelings, we bring goodness, light, and love into the world. These are the activities of righteousness. It is through us, responding to the goodness within us, that the Lord's light is shed throughout the world. We are the angels! We can be eagerly involved in doing many good things.

We can't sit back and complain about how evil the world has

become if we are not committed to being a force for good. It is amazing to watch a person who steps up and begins to do good things. Their whole demeanor changes. Discouragement flees. They radiate light and love in a transforming way.

My life's motto is from Mahatma Gandhi. I include it at the end of all my e-mails, and it expresses my feelings exactly: "*You* must be the change you wish to see in the world."[2]

I like to read the sentence over and over, emphasizing a different word each time. "You *must* be the change you wish to see in the world." "You must *be* the change you wish to see in the world." This is such a powerful message.

Each of us can be that person. Each of us can create that change.

How can you find ways to serve? First, think about your interests or skills. Are you good with children? Do you have business skills? Do you organize well? Do you like the idea of helping at a food bank?

Then you can begin to research. The Internet is an invaluable tool. One website I like to recommend is 1-800-Volunteer.org. Simply enter where you live, some key words of what you want to do, click the magical word "Volunteer," and all kinds of opportunities will pop up.

Next, pay attention! Many communities have an organization that serves as a clearinghouse for service opportunities. In our area, it's called "San Diego Cares" and you sign up on a list and they send information on upcoming opportunities. Or you can begin with your own PTA. Walk into your city offices and ask what you can do to help. Look in the front of the Yellow Pages and you'll often find listings for community groups. Ask other people what they're doing. Pray for direction.

What else can you do? What about some of these simple and easy ideas:

- Make dinner for someone in need and go deliver it!
- Donate your used books to your children's school library or to a homeless shelter.
- Donate blood or plasma.
- Organize a Neighborhood Watch group.
- Adopt a park, highway, or beach to keep clean.
- Volunteer with the Girl Scouts or Boy Scouts.
- Write your testimony in a Book of Mormon and give it to the missionaries.
- Make quilts and donate them to the local fire station or homeless shelter.
- Leave a snack and a note of appreciation in your mailbox for the mail carrier.
- For an entire day, greet every single person with a smile and a hello!

In the Appendix of this book there is a list of even more suggestions for good things to do. There is *so much* good we can do. Just go where your heart leads you and start!

Imagine if every person on your street, in your neighborhood, in your city were to donate one hour of service per month. That could be 5,000 to 10,000 hours per month or more and maybe more than 100,000 hours per year! What a tremendous difference that could make in the world. Can you imagine the news broadcasts? Reporters would be saying, "Hmm, something is happening across the country, and we can't explain it. Thousands of people are doing good spontaneously. We don't know why, but we do know that amazing things are happening!" Now *that* is a news broadcast I'd like to hear!

But to get there, each of us must take action. That action will be as unique as we are. And if each of us can do a little something every day, the impact will be tremendous. We can and we must be the change we wish to see in the world, and we can start right now!

CHAPTER 6

Light the Way, Lead the Way

*"To give light to them that sit in darkness
and in the shadow of death, to guide our feet
into the way of peace."*

—Luke 1:79

I am so inspired by the stories of great leaders. I think of President Thomas S. Monson and his work of love that has continued throughout his entire life. I think of Florence Nightingale, Albert Schweitzer, and Mother Teresa. I think of all the many men and women who have led in love.

And so we come to the final step in standing up: leading others in taking action.

I am convinced that there is no real difference in skills, talents, or abilities between someone who is a leader and someone who is not. The only difference is that a leader *does* something. Leaders take action. That's pretty much it.

When a leader drives through a pothole, they grab their phone and make a call to get it fixed. When a leader sees someone in need, they take action.

A leader has the confidence to stand alone, the courage to make tough decisions, and the compassion to listen to the needs of others.

A leader doesn't stand around wondering what other people will think of them. A leader is willing to take action. That takes courage. It takes guts to see something and say, "I'm going to do something about that!" They have that confidence to step up. And, often, that first step is one they take alone.

A leader listens. A true leader listens well and hears a person's needs.

So many around us have good hearts and want to do good. So many around us are willing to help if they just knew what to do and how. It is so easy to lead people in doing good.

We can begin, very simply, by leading ourselves. That may sound silly, but it's real, and frankly, the meetings are a lot shorter when there's just one person involved! We can start leading ourselves to do good with all the things that we have been discussing in this book. Choosing to help. Reaching out to others. Praying. Our actions can begin a ripple of goodness than can touch the lives of many.

As you begin to live a life of service, you will begin to glow. You won't be able to help yourself. You will begin to radiate love and light, and others will notice. They will ask you what's different.

And then you can lead others. Tell them what you're doing and ask them to join you. It's that simple.

We can expand our influence to those around us quite easily. We just have to communicate with them. In this age of the Internet and social media, our ability to communicate and lead is growing daily.

Years ago, I began "Merrilee's List." This was simply a list of e-mail addresses that I had collected. I would communicate with friends on my e-mail list and tell them what projects I was working on. They would ask if they could help. The list began to grow . . . and grow!

When the wildfires hit our area in 2004, I led the efforts to provide relief to those who had lost their homes. My list grew and grew, and the miracles began to happen. I would send out an e-mail message about a fire victim family who needed a set of bunk beds, and within hours, I'd have several responses from people willing to donate bunk beds. I'd send out an e-mail that we were collecting gift cards and gift cards would start showing up on my porch.

I once wrote a little story about that porch.

Our Magic Porch—There Is Plenty

I have a magic porch. It's just a small redbrick porch—nothing out of the ordinary. But it's magic. I call it the "Magic Porch of Plenty."

My porch is magic because miracles happen there all the time. Unseen, anonymous miracles.

Such a miracle happened many times this month. I live in Poway, California (north of San Diego), and we lost ninety homes in the Witch Creek fire of 2007. This was the second horrible wildfire to strike our city within four years. This was also the second time I volunteered as the Fire Relief Coordinator. After receiving the names and information for the families involved, I put out a request to more than 1,000 of my close, personal friends who have managed to get on my e-mail distribution list one way or the other.

"Help! These families need your help! We need gift cards for food, gas, clothing—anything. Get them to me as fast as you can!"

And then the miracles began to happen. My porch began to sprout gift cards! We had to routinely go out and lift up the mat and scour the porch for gift cards tucked all over. And it didn't stop there! Boxes came from out of state with donations. Quilts spontaneously appeared. It was amazing! But not surprising to us.

The Magic Porch of Plenty has even spread. Marta's family had lost their home in the fire and virtually everything they owned. But she called me one day. "Guess what?" she said. "Our old Suburban didn't burn in the fire. We drove it around and it works great. We want to donate it to a family in need."

Well, just that day I had received an e-mail from a woman in our ward who is going through a divorce and has three kids at home. Someone had hit her car on Halloween and totaled her car. I contacted both women and lined up the exchange.

My ward sister recounts what happened later. "Here I stood on what was left of her porch surrounded by ashes from her burned-out home. And here she was giving me her car—the only thing that survived intact. I don't understand that kind of gift. It was truly amazing."

Marta came by my home and stood on my porch. "Oh, it felt so wonderful to be the one receiving the tears of gratitude!" she said. "It's been so hard being the one crying with gratitude all the time. It felt so good to be able to give!"

The Lord knew that one sister needed to give and one sister needed to receive.

Over the years, my children have gathered homemade dolls for fire families, T-shirt dresses for African children, envelopes with cash to donate, homemade quilts and blankets, medical supplies, quilts for firefighters, suits for homeless women, books for children, and on and on and on. All anonymously dropped on our porch. The magic porch.

You see, we are so very blessed to have a porch that

grows love. It has served for decades as a point where love is given and love is delivered.

Somehow I think Heavenly Father has a porch like ours. We bring our gifts to His porch—our time, our efforts, our donations of love. And He gives them to those in need, together with His love, and that makes our small gifts perfect. Yes, He too, has a magic porch. And there we can give and receive love. And His porch has plenty for all.

Day after day, "Merrilee's List" produced amazing little miracles. And it grew and grew. Over the years, the list has grown to more than a thousand people. And on that list are people who have their own list of more than a thousand others. Who knows how many people we can reach?

The power that circle of influence can have has been remarkable. With this group, we've changed city policy, blessed lives, and made a huge difference. And it all started with one e-mail.

A Call for Donations

Each of us can develop leadership in his or her own way. My son Connor is a web developer and political activist and has been developing his sphere of influence since he was a young boy. He just turned thirty years old, and he has already gathered thousands of contacts with e-mail lists, Facebook, Twitter, and his blog, and he is using his influence to lead as well as to serve.

One day we were both online and he sent me a link to an article. A young bishop in Visalia, California, had been shot and killed by a gunman in church on Sunday. I was stunned by the news. I immediately began to pray for the family. I stood up and walked to my kitchen, and by the time I got there, thoughts were racing through my head.

My first thoughts, of course, were for the bishop's family. I could not imagine what they were experiencing and how their lives had changed. I thought about the shooter, wondering what pain had been in his life that would cause him to do such a thing. I thought about how his own family would be affected by his actions.

My next thought was that simple question: "What can I do about this?"

I thought, *I can donate $20.* Such an odd thought. I immediately thought, *Oh, I can donate more . . . but how?* And then my brain went into high gear with ideas. For me, that is usually a sure sign that I am no longer in control and the Spirit is beginning to work.

I reached for the phone and dialed my son, who was living in Utah. "Connor, we have to do something," I said. "This family is going to need help. And they are going to need money. I want to donate to them. And as people read this story, they will want to help and want to donate as well. We need to get on the Internet immediately and set up an easy way for people to donate money. That way the people who want to help can do so immediately."

"I'm on it, Mom," he replied. It was almost as if our brains were working in unison. We were thinking the same thoughts and working in the same direction. Connor is very web-savvy and within one hour, he had set up a Pledgie account at Pledgie.com for people to donate to the family via Paypal. We were talking constantly, thinking of what else we needed to do.

I remember he said that he was setting the goal at $2,000.

I said, "Oh, honey, we can raise more than that. I think we can raise $10,000 for the family." But we left the goal low for the time being.

As soon as I could, I sent out an e-mail to Merrilee's List. Connor sent out an e-mail to Connor's List. Then Connor hit the online social media sites and posted on his blog. We also notified all the press outlets we could reach. And then we watched and waited.

Meanwhile, I called my bishop and asked him if he could get the contact information for the Church leaders in the Visalia area. We needed to reach the family as quickly as we could to tell them who we were, that we were legitimately trying to help, and not to worry. We needed to know how to get the money to them directly and safely. My bishop went to work.

And then things started to happen.

Within hours, we'd raised $5,000. Then we got a phone call from a donor who wanted to donate $5,000 anonymously. We raised the limit at Pledgie.com.

The next day, the story began to hit the media, both in California and Utah. We were able to talk to the stake president and assure him that all was well. He also talked to our church leaders to make sure Connor and I were good, trustworthy folk. The family was contacted and steps were set up to get the money to them directly.

And the donations kept coming. Ten dollars, twenty, one hundred dollars. The donations began to spread in a wave from west to east and even to other countries.

The goal kept rising as the donations kept coming—$10,000, $20,000, $30,000. It was unbelievable. I said, "Connor, we have to raise $60,000. There are six little boys who have lost their father. They will need $10,000 each to go on a mission. Do you think it will happen?"

By the next week, more than $70,000 had been raised for the family. People literally all over the world had been touched by the tragic story and had taken action.

Connor and I learned a lot in that experience. First, we need to respond when we feel caring. That is always our guiding principle. Second, leaders can make it easy for others to respond by showing them how. And they will. They absolutely will respond. Third, the Lord provides angels all over the world. This world is filled with good, caring, loving people who will stand up and do good.

The Power of One

Leadership can begin with one person and then it can spread. Our power for influence is tremendous. It doesn't always take a big service project or a big idea—it can begin as something small, and as we lead and influence others, it can grow.

The power of one is immense.

One person can change a home.

One person can change a community.

One person can change the world.

You can change your home. You know that. You do it every day.

And you can change a community. It's not that hard. Just speak up or help out a little.

And you can indeed change the world. Every single good thing you do can change the world. I have met many people whose influence has spread, people who have done amazing things.

Leadership can be as easy as a twelve-year-old boy speaking before a city council or a school board and leading hundreds in the pursuit of truth. Leadership can begin with a young man standing up in a crowd and saying, "I'm collecting donations!" It can begin by you simply telling your neighbors that you're collecting jackets for needy schoolchildren. It can begin with you sending an e-mail or posting a note on Facebook and inviting others to join with you in service.

And please know that when you stand up, others will stand with you. At first, it may seem that you are alone. But others will join you. They may be friends, family, and associates who assist you. Or they may be unseen helpers. I am convinced that as we stand up to do good and fight evil, we are surrounded and supported by those on the other side of the veil who are involved and supportive of our efforts.

The Lord is mindful of what we do, and so are His angels.

President Gordon B. Hinckley said it so well:

> The tide of evil flows. Today it has become a veritable flood. Most of us, living somewhat sheltered lives, have little idea of the vast dimensions of it. . . . God give us the strength, the wisdom, the faith, the courage as citizens to stand in opposition to these and to let our voices be heard in defense of those virtues which, when practiced in the past, made men and nations strong, and which, when neglected, brought them to decay.
>
> God lives. He is our strength and our helper. As we strive, we shall discover that legions of good men and women will join with us. Let us begin now.[1]

> Are these perilous times? They are. But there is no need to fear. We can have peace in our hearts and peace in our homes. We can be an influence for good in this world, every one of us.
>
> Let our voices be heard.[2]

President Thomas S. Monson testified of the same truth:

> As the winds of change swirl around us and the moral fiber of society continues to disintegrate before our very eyes, may we remember the Lord's precious promise to those who trust in Him: "Fear thou not; for I am with thee: be not dismayed; for I am thy God: I will strengthen thee; yea, I will help thee; yea, I will uphold thee with the right hand of my righteousness." [Isaiah 41:10.]
>
> What a promise![3]

We *can* be a tremendous influence for good and light and love as we stand up. We can withstand evil and speak in defense of truth. We can create in ourselves lives of goodness and charity. And we can lead others in standing up for good wherever we are.

The Lord is calling upon us to help. The clarion call of a prophet of God rings in our ears: "I think the Lord would say to us, 'Rise, and stand upon thy feet, and speak up for truth and goodness and decency and virtue.'"[4]

May we all rise and stand up and do so together.

Appendix

To receive the following in electronic format or to respond to this book, e-mail Merrilee at maboyack@gmail.com. You can connect with Merrilee at MerrileeBoyack.com, or on Facebook at http://www.facebook.com/merrileeboyack, or on Twitter at Twitter.com/MerrBoyack.

Stand Up and Speak Out

- Meet personally with each of your political representatives. Let them get to know you.

- E-mail or call your political representatives regularly about the issues you are passionate about. Be respectful but firm in your message.

- Write a letter to a newspaper or magazine editor on important issues. Encourage your children and teenagers to write letters also!

- Vote in every election.

- Get involved in your political party. Study the issues, and stay informed.
- Sign a petition, either online or on paper—better yet, collect signatures yourself!
- Write an op-ed article for your local newspaper.
- Visit your children's schools and pay attention to the curriculum. Read what your children read. Be involved in their classrooms and with their teachers. Let the teachers know your standards and ask them to alert you if anything comes up that may violate those standards.
- Develop an e-mail list of like-minded individuals. Communicate with those on your list about issues that are important to you or about opportunities for service.
- Write a Facebook or blog post or tweet about something you believe in.
- Identify a problem in your community, find out who is in charge of that area, and ask what you can do to help fix the problem.
- Attend and speak at your local meetings. Anyone can speak about anything at the beginning of these public meetings so use that time to change things!
- Join Toastmasters and learn the skill of public speaking.
- Pray for your leaders—local, state, and federal. Fast for them as well.
- Stand up and speak out, then support others who stand up and speak out!

"Feed My Sheep"

- Donate to a food bank once a month.
- Make dinner for someone in need and go deliver it!

- Invite your neighbors over for a potluck dinner. Make it an annual tradition.

- As a family, serve dinner one night at a soup kitchen.

- Organize a community garden and donate the harvest to the food bank.

- Deliver sack lunches to a homeless shelter.

- Volunteer to make a meal for the families at the Ronald McDonald House.

- Deliver food to seniors with the Meals on Wheels program.

- Donate breakfast items to your school—cereal bars, granola bars, juice boxes—for the kids who can't pay for school meals.

- Pay for the person behind you in a drive-thru fast-food restaurant.

Collect and Donate

- Add $5 to your church contribution and designate it for "Humanitarian Aid."

- Recycle your cans and bottles and donate the money to a charity.

- Donate your used books to your children's school library or to a homeless shelter.

- Donate your magazines to a shelter.

- Collect donation items for Deseret Industries or the Salvation Army.

- Donate blood or plasma.

- Donate hair to LocksofLove.org.

- Sign up to be an organ donor.

- Donate cleaning products or supplies for families in need.

- Collect and donate CDs and DVDs for shelters, hospitals, or school libraries.
- Keep the Law of Finite Hangers: We have a rule in our house that for each closet there is a set number of hangers, never more. When we buy something new, we donate something so the number of hangers remains the same.

"Love Thy Neighbor"

- Collect gently used children's toys. Clean them and donate them to families at a battered women's shelter, a homeless shelter, or low-income housing areas.
- Volunteer in a school classroom or at the library. Host a "reading time" for children. Bring a "thank-you" treat to the school librarian or custodian.
- Become a mentor for an adolescent.
- Read books to the blind.
- Visit patients at your local hospital.
- Volunteer to serve on a city committee.
- Organize a Neighborhood Watch group.
- Offer free childcare to those attending community or school meetings.
- Organize a community blood drive.
- Call the school district and ask if you can help clean up the school grounds. Take hoes, shovels, rakes, gloves, and do some real clean-up work.
- Plant a tree.
- Adopt a park, highway, or beach to keep clean.
- Help with repairs at a local shelter or church.

- Organize an emergency preparedness plan for your neighborhood.
- Offer to babysit your neighbor's children for an evening.

Join the Club

Remember to always contact the organization before you begin a project to see if they have specific needs.

- Contact Habitat for Humanity and volunteer.
- Volunteer with the Red Cross. Take a class in CPR.
- Contact your local service club (Rotary, Soroptimists, Elks, Lions, Kiwanis, etc.) and volunteer.
- Celebrate national "Make a Difference Day" on the fourth Saturday in October with a family service project.
- Offer to be a Big Brother or a Big Sister.
- If you're a retired businessperson, volunteer for a group like SCORE.
- Volunteer with the Girl Scouts or Boy Scouts.
- Volunteer to help at the Special Olympics.
- Join your PTA—even if you don't have kids or if they're grown.
- Contact LDS Social Services to volunteer to be a foster parent.

Share Your Spirit

- Write your testimony in a Book of Mormon and give it to the missionaries.
- Volunteer at the bishops' storehouse.

Make Something Special

- Make quilts and donate them to the local fire station or homeless shelter.
- Sew dresses made out of T-shirts for girls.
- Crochet caps or afghans for babies. Make baby layettes and donate to local Life Choices Counseling centers.
- Make placemats for nursing homes or soup kitchens.
- Make birthday cards for seniors or those in nursing homes.
- Assemble school supply kits. Make a simple backpack and fill it with a book and other supplies.
- Assemble beauty kits of lotion, makeup, and jewelry for women at a shelter.
- Assemble hygiene kits at the Humanitarian Center.

Honor Those Who Have Served Our Country

- Write letters or cards to military servicemen or servicewomen.
- Leave a snack and a note of appreciation in your mailbox for the mail carrier.
- Invite a serviceman over for dinner or to celebrate the holidays.
- Plan a Memorial Day or Veterans Day program to recognize veterans in your neighborhood.

Acts of Love, Acts of Service

- For an entire day, greet every single person with a smile and a hello!
- Take a bouquet of flowers to a single mom or dad.
- Give out twenty hugs a day.

- Write a thank-you note to the five most important people in your life.
- Plant flowers anonymously for friends and neighbors.
- Clean the house and yard of an elderly neighbor.
- Volunteer at a local nursing home. Visit with the residents, sing songs with them, play the piano for them, interview them about their life history, offer to conduct a craft session, or bring sugar-free treats.

You Can Do It!

- Make a service jar and fill it with slips of paper of service ideas and your favorite candy—do a service, take a candy.
- Wear a "Good Works" charm bracelet—do a service, add a charm.
- Save your change throughout the year and just before Christmas convert the coins to bills and donate the money to a charity or a family in need.
- Have a charity birthday party. Invite guests to bring toys or clothes that can be donated.
- Organize a "service sale." Offer a range of services, and the money people spend is donated to a designated charity.
- Participate in a run/walk/bike ride for charity.
- Have a car wash, yard sale, or bake sale, or open a lemonade stand. Donate the proceeds to charity.
- Surf online for ideas of good things you could do. Search for the words that touch you the most: "children with leukemia," "abandoned animals," or "wounded warriors." Visit DoOneNiceThing.org, DoSomething.org, EveryMondayMatters.com, or CharityNavigator.org. There are so many ways to help!

Notes

CHAPTER 1: DECIDE TO BE A GIVER

1. "Of Experience," in *The Essays of Michel de Montaigne*, trans. Charles Cotton, ed. William Carew Hazlitt (South Australia: University of Adelaide, 2010), http://ebooks.adelaide.edu.au/m/montaigne/michel/essays/book3.13.html.
2. Gordon B. Hinckley, "Stand Up for Truth," in *Brigham Young University 1996–97 Speeches* (Provo: Brigham Young University, 1997), 22.
3. Henry B. Eyring, "A Witness," *Ensign*, November 2011, 68.
4. Henry B. Eyring, *To Draw Closer to God: A Collection of Discourses* (Salt Lake City: Deseret Book, 1997), 87–88; emphasis in original.
5. Linda McCullough Moore, "Generous Hearts," *Family Circle*, April 1, 2005, 144.

CHAPTER 2: STANDING UP

1. Helen Keller, *My Religion* (San Diego, CA: The Book Tree, 2007), 162.

2. Gordon B. Hinckley, "Stand Up for Truth," in *Brigham Young University 1996–97 Speeches* (Provo: Brigham Young University, 1997), 26; emphasis added.

3. Gordon B. Hinckley, "In Opposition to Evil," *Ensign,* September 2004, 3–4; emphasis added.

4. See Dallin H. Oaks, "Good, Better, Best," *Ensign,* November 2007, 104–8.

5. "The Family: A Proclamation to the World," *Ensign,* November 1995, 102; emphasis added.

6. James J. Hamula, "Winning the War against Evil," *Ensign,* November 2008, 51.

7. Mohandas Gandhi, in John C. Maxwell, *Talent Is Never Enough: Discover the Choices That Will Take You Beyond Your Talent* (Nashville, TN: Thomas Nelson, 2011), 16.

8. Gordon B. Hinckley, "Pursue the Steady Course," *Ensign,* January 2005, 4.

9. M. Russell Ballard, "Standing for Truth and Right," *Ensign,* November 1997, 38.

10. Hinckley, "In Opposition to Evil," 5–6; emphasis added.

CHAPTER 3: WITHSTAND EVIL

1. Gordon B. Hinckley, "Stand Up for Truth," in *Brigham Young University 1996–97 Speeches* (Provo: Brigham Young University, 1997), 24.

2. Gordon B. Hinckley, "Pursue the Steady Course," *Ensign,* January 2005, 6.

3. Gordon B. Hinckley, "The Quest for Excellence," *Ensign,* September 1999, 4–5.

4. Thomas S. Monson, "Dare to Stand Alone," *Ensign,* November 2011, 60.

5. Richard G. Scott, "Be a Shining Light," *BYU Magazine* (Fall 2011): 3.

6. Thomas S. Monson, "Three Goals to Guide You," *Ensign,* November 2007, 120.

7. Private letter in possession of author.

8. Monson, "Three Goals to Guide You," 118–19.

9. Elaine S. Dalton, "Love Her Mother," *Ensign,* November 2011, 77–78; emphasis in original.

10. Monson, "Three Goals to Guide You," 120.

11. Private communication with author.

CHAPTER 4: RICH IN GOOD WORKS

1. Howard W. Hunter, "To the Women of the Church," *Ensign,* November 1992, 96.

2. Vanja Y. Watkins, "I Will Be Valiant," in *Children's Songbook* (Salt Lake City: The Church of Jesus Christ of Latter-day Saints, 1989), 162.

3. Gordon B. Hinckley, "The Times in Which We Live," *Ensign,* November 2001, 74.

4. Carl B. Cook, "It Is Better to Look Up," *Ensign,* November 2011, 35.

5. Thomas S. Monson, "Heavenly Homes, Forever Families," *Ensign,* June 2006, 102.

6. Russell T. Osguthorpe, "When Love Is Why," *BYU Magazine* (Fall 2011): 53, 55, 56.

CHAPTER 5: DO THE GREATEST GOOD

1. http://www.wordreference.com/definition/anxiously.

2. The original quote is "We need to be the change we wish to see in the world," as reported by Arun Gandhi, who was quoting his grandfather. Michael W. Potts, "Arun Gandhi Shares the Mahatma's Message," in *India-West* (San Leandro, Calif.), vol. 27, no. 13 (1 February 2002): A34; see also "Arun Gandhi on Terrorism, Nonviolence, and Gandhi," *Global Tribe,* www.pbs.org/kcet/globaltribe/voices/voi_gandhi.html.

CHAPTER 6: LIGHT THE WAY, LEAD THE WAY

1. Gordon B. Hinckley, "In Opposition to Evil," *Ensign,* September 2004, 6.

2. Gordon B. Hinckley, "The Times in Which We Live," *Ensign*, November 2001, 74.

3. Thomas S. Monson, "Stand in Holy Places," *Ensign*, November 2011, 86.

4. Hinckley, "In Opposition to Evil," 6.

Index

About the Author

MERRILEE BOYACK is a popular speaker at BYU Education Week and at Time Out for Women conferences. She is an estate-planning attorney who conducts her part-time law practice from her home in Poway, California, where she also serves as a member of the city council. Merrilee and her husband are the parents of four sons.